The Real

Guide to Life
as a Couple

Praeclarus Press, LLC

2504 Sweetgum Lane

Amarillo, Texas 79124 USA

806-367-9950

www.PraeclarusPress.com

DISCLAIMER

The information contained in this publication is advisory only and is not intended to replace sound clinical judgment or individualized patient care. The author disclaims all warranties, whether expressed or implied, including any warranty as the quality, accuracy, safety, or suitability of this information for any particular purpose.

ISBN: 978-1-946665-19-5

Illustrations: Sid Azri

Cover Design: Ken Tackett

Developmental Editing: Kathleen Kendall-Tackett

Copy Editing: Chris Tackett

Layout & Design: Nelly Murariu

The *Real*
Guide to Life as a Couple

STEPHANIE AZRI, PhD

Illustrated by Sid Azri

Praeclarus Press, LLC
©2018 Stephanie Azri. All rights reserved.

www.PraeclarusPress.com

FOREWORD

As a psychosexual and couple therapist, people come to me to improve their relationships. Through my work, I have witnessed a need for enhanced communication skills between the couple; the ability to actively listen and demonstrate listening by putting what our partner says into our own words. These important skills form the basis of the first part of *The REAL Guide to Life as a Couple*. It is these enhanced skills which help "scaffold" the relationship—the structure which helps support the relationship. Building blocks help lay the foundation, and these are often forgotten with time. It is the small, everyday things we do with, and for, our partners which help scaffold or support the relationship. When a relationship is well-scaffolded, then it is possible to begin discussing the bigger issues. Our relationships do not happen in a vacuum. We are surrounded by family and friends; we hold hopes, dreams, and shared goals. *The REAL Guide to Life as a Couple* addresses these topics perfectly.

One of the greatest obstacles to healthy and happy relationship I witness at times is the role social media plays. Couples engagement with social media can be distancing and isolating. These two words, distance and isolation, are not friends of a relationship. In fact, it is the foundation of no relationship. A relationship brings a couple together. Stephanie's guide provides a framework for couples to work through these issues and develop healthy relationship skills at the same time. Then, the section on sex and intimacy addresses aspects developed through a couple's lifespan. In my work, I often find couples experience difficulty talking about sex. There is not a shared language with sex; we have our own ideas about sex, and when our partner speaks about sex, we often hear through our own sexual lives. In working through the exercises and activities in *The REAL Guide*, couples can develop greater communication skills, and an ability to explore their ideas about sex before developing a shared understanding of a couple's sexuality.

When I first met Stephanie at a workshop five years ago, she brought energy to the course and a unique way of breaking tasks down into simpler forms. This skill is something I believe is a necessity with any therapist; our clients need small, manageable, and achievable tasks. *The REAL Guide to Life as a Couple* does this perfectly. Stephanie takes a series of complex tasks and brings to her readers a series of comprehensible narratives, along with activities which build a couple's skills and abilities to address the difficult questions. Each chapter is laid in a clear and easy-to-follow format. The strength of *The REAL Guide* as a self-help book is how Stephanie develops a couple's skills as they move through it. The use of humor also makes for easy reading.

Many of the exercises are tried. Stephanie sought feedback on *The REAL Guide* during its development with real people—not necessarily professionals. To add to this strength, I have used a number of exercises with couples. For example, I used the Positive Communications in Relationships as featured in Chapter Two. I also found the chapter on family and friends very applicable and user-friendly. All in all, Stephanie has produced a book which is easy to read, with exercises that are fun and based in the real world for real couples. I welcome a book that is accessible and can bring hope to a couple. Although nothing can replace the work of a therapist, not all couples need a professional all the time. With a book like *this one*, can meet many of couples' needs. I look forward to being able to recommend *The REAL Guide to Life as a Couple* to my clients.

Dr. Christopher Fox
🌐 www.sexlifetherapy.com.au

Dr. Christopher Fox is a Psychosexual and Relationship Therapist based in Melbourne, Australia. He is also the Director of Sex Life Therapy. Dr. Christopher is highly recognized in the sex therapy community, nationally and internationally. He coordinates the Psychosexual Therapy Postgraduate Program at the University of Sydney. He is the Immediate Past Chairperson of the Society of Australian Sexologists. Dr. Christopher is often quoted for his expert opinion in the media. On the international stage, Dr. Christopher is an Executive Member of the Asia-Oceania Federation of Sexology and the Associate-Secretary for the Asia-Pacific region with the World Association for Sexual Health.

ACKNOWLEDGMENTS

It is with great excitement that I present to you *The REAL Guide to Life as a Couple.* For those of you who have purchased my other books in the past, this will be a breath of fresh air, for this book is a much lighter read. For those couples who have seen me in a therapeutic setting, this will be exactly like hearing my voice in the background, and you will recognize a lot of the things we have been talking about in therapy. I hope that you enjoy my trademark bluntness and find the tips in this book useful.

Before I start, I wanted to talk about relationships. Relationships are broad and can include professional, familial, sexual, romantic, social, and platonic partnerships. These may be between friends, relatives, or work colleagues, as well as strangers that cross our paths. In this book, we are talking about relationships that are romantic (or so we hope) and between two people who are in a serious partnership (or want to be). I am talking to all of you. Males, females, heterosexuals, and gay couples who, as regular people, may benefit from relationship tips to take their relationship to the next level. While the illustrations may include a combination of males/females, and show one gender or the other working for and against my golden advice, leave any assumptions behind right now. There is no hidden meaning behind them. We simply hoped to provide you with funny characters to go along with some sound therapeutic suggestions, and we send our love and respect to all couples, regardless of their gender, sexuality, race, culture, or religion.

Another important fact I wanted to touch on, is that in a "normal" loving relationship, we are almost always *equally* responsible for improving our communication and our connection. I make a point in my therapy sessions to remind my clients that unless it is about making sense of it, I don't want to hear about the other person's downfalls. WE are responsible for our behaviors, thoughts, and feelings, and so, in this book, you will find that I will always talk about what YOU can control and change as opposed to discussing how you could change your partner. However, if you are in a relationship that is violent, threatening, or abusive in any way, please seek help. None of the advice in this book alone can fix domestic violence, and so, if you believe you might be in one of these relationships, seek support and advice from a trained therapist (individually as opposed to with your partner). I send my love and encourage you to find the strength to speak up. For everyone else, be brave and enjoy the ride towards a happier relationship.

On a lighter note, I would like to thank all the people who made this book possible. Thank you, Praeclarus Press, for a fantastic partnership and showing a clear passion for the work that I am doing with women, couples, and families. Thank you to my husband for providing the book with illustrations, and thank you for being my partner in crime for the last couple of decades; we make a good team. Thank you to my beta readers for your opinions and advice, in particular, Kimbali Wild, who has read this book from start to finish and provided me feedback on it. I appreciate your support and guidance over the last year. Finally, thank you to all my clients and Facebook followers who provided me with the anecdotes throughout the book. Your funny perspectives have added much depth to *The REAL Guide to Life as a Couple*.

In closing, dear readers, I have provided you with serious relationship advice, amidst lots of fun exercises and challenges. These are designed to get you thinking and get you talking with your partner. By no means is this book trying to give you all the tools and solutions you may need over time, but there is hope that it will give you enough insight to challenge you and encourage you in your relationship development. The "truth or dare" section is designed to challenge you with practical exercises that are non-threatening and enlightening. I hope you find the examples and anecdotes funny but please, oh please, if you ever wonder which examples are the right ones to mirror, don't hesitate to contact me! I would love to hear from you.

Yours in relationships,

Dr. Stephanie Azri

🌐 www.stephanieazri.com
🔲 www.facebook.com/stephanieazriauthor

CONTENTS

PART ONE

Are You Ready?

GETTING TO KNOW YOUR PERSONALITIES

We are wired with lots of differences. Some of our personality traits will be noticed quickly, while others will take time to come up to the surface. As you get to know your partner, you may notice a temperament that belongs to them. For example, you may notice your partner avoiding social situations, or needing to sleep much less than you.

We may associate the term compatibility with temperament. If you think about it, we all have likes and dislikes, as well as traits we could, and would never, put up with. Have you ever imagined your perfect partner? If you have, just abandon the idea right now; he or she does not exist. Jokes asides, picture the following scenarios. You have always pictured yourself with a traveling companion, and you end up in a relationship with someone who refuses to leave the house. Even worse, imagine that you are an animal lover and meet your perfect man or woman, and find out that they despise everything about these creatures. Who would you give up first? We understand how personalities, temperament, likes and dislikes play a great part in compatibility. Before we continue discussing long-term compatibility, let's further explore temperaments.

In short, things that define us, inbuilt characteristics make up what we call our temperament, our nature, our disposition, or our personality, if you will. While we could include lots of information in defining personality and temperament, here are some of the domains that might help you understand your partner's disposition (and yours):

> *My husband and I are very different. I need at least 8 to 10 hours of sleep a night, and he can stay up pretty much all night and still function. I'm also a bit of an introvert, and he's a social butterfly. We always knew we were poles apart in temperament, but it became more obvious when we had a son who was exactly like me and a daughter who was exactly like her father!*
>
> *There was no denying our inbuilt personalities!*

Activity Level

How much activity do you do throughout the day (beyond your job or scheduled activities)? Some of us are naturally sedentary while others prefer to move all the time. This goes beyond choice and extends to how people can cope sitting down (long reading sessions, for example), or how quickly a person loses their mind after a time of running around. Very casually, if your partner is more of a slouch than they are Indiana Jones, you might have some difficulty in convincing him that a complete weekend of gardening is an exciting prospect.

Predictability

How predictable are your or your partner's routines? Do you anticipate meals, bathroom breaks, or sleeping habits without a shadow of a doubt? What happens when you or your partner's routine is disrupted? Is it more "who cares" or "who dares?" Someone's need for predictability is an important part of their character needs, and will influence how they cope with change.

Tolerance

Essentially, how much can you handle before you lose it? Our tolerance levels range from low to high. Some of us will be able to manage quite a bit before giving in to frustration, while others won't take much to set them off. You can see how this would have a big impact on how you or your partner manage situations and this would be important to know in your partnership, particularly before your spouse has a full-blown meltdown for the first time.

Mood Type

We all have met positive individuals who look at the bright side of things no matter what, and others who tend to sit on the critical edge. Now, while I admit we might be born with a tendency to be positive or negative, I would be going against my professional opinion if I didn't add that I genuinely believe that people can learn to become more positive with good therapy. But for the sake of this section, I will only highlight that if you meet someone who tends to be on the negative side, it would be unrealistic to imagine that a marriage later, they would completely change and become the most positive person on the planet.

> " *I am the mother of five children, and of course, I love them all. But one of them was born with a gift. My "ray of sunshine," as I call him, is the most positive, happy, encouraging, and hopeful little boy I have ever come across in my life. There was no teaching him to be positive. He just was.*
>
> *Someone like that will make an amazing and supportive partner.*
>
> *Bias? What do you mean I'm biased?*

Adaptability/Flexibility

How much effort does it take you to adapt to a new job, new persons, or new situations? Are you or your partner people who tend to approach new events head-on, or would you rather stick with the well-known and good old routines? Highly adaptable personalities will love unplanned dates and last-minute changes, while others would feel a surge of anxiety or annoyance at the poorly planned get together when the cinema is suddenly closed up for renovations on your third rendezvous.

Persistence

This is one of my favorite traits. People have often said to me, "you must be smart to have done this or that," and I always remind them that it's not about being smart but about being tenacious. Persistence is about having a clear idea or plan and following through, despite the adversities, and looking for alternative solutions, rather than giving up early. If your partner is persistent, this may mean a lifetime of successes. However, it may also mean his refusal to give up on building furniture at 2 am, when you are to wake up the next day at 6 am to go to work.

Introvert vs. Extrovert

Generally, introverts prefer limited social contacts and some emotional distance between them and others. They tend to be quieter than extroverts and are naturally reserved. Too much attention could upset the introvert, who may come across as shy, guarded, and sometimes even vigilant. On the other hand, extroverts make awesome party companions, who generally love being the class clown and the center of attention. They tend to make friends rather quickly but may not analyze information as deeply as their introvert counterparts. This is another trait that will not change. If your partner is an extrovert when you meet him, don't expect him or her to tone it down later, just because this is what you need. Rather, accept that this is a trait that he or she will keep for life, and become aware of what this means for you as a partner.

Now, these are inbuilt, and so far, in theory, pretty easy to adapt to. The key is to understand what these mean in practice. Using one of my previous examples, imagine your anti-animal lover with a very intolerant temperament and a tendency to sit on the irritable side, as opposed to your anti-animal lover who is adaptable and flexible. Though they are both extremely different from you, the odds are that one would refuse to compromise while the other would, or may even start becoming familiar with animals over time.

I Get It, But How Do I Work with It?

Alright, so by now, you may have noticed certain *qualities* in your partner, which may or may not irritate you like crazy! Before you got married or moved in together, you may not have noticed them, may have thought that you could live with them, or Heaven forbid, you thought you would *change* your partner (insert shock horror).

Let me stop you right here. We cannot change our temperament. Most of what we are discussing in this chapter will be here to stay and would be almost impossible to change. And bluntly, why would you want to? It is not better or worse to be an introvert or an extrovert, or active versus static. It's more about compatibility and acceptance rather than right/wrong.

If you are in a new relationship, ask yourself whether you could see yourself with this person's permanent personality traits in ten years. If the answer is yes, rejoice. That's round one of the relationship rollercoaster out of the way. If the answer is no, then ask yourself what this is about? Is this about control (wanting your partner to fit a certain mold), about perception (assuming one trait is better than another), or is this about your needs (what is it that *you* need to feel happy, safe, fulfilled etc.)?

For the sake of this exercise, here are a couple of examples:

You receive a text from another couple, inviting you over for dinner at the last minute. You can already smell the aroma of Asian fusion from here and have prepacked your new board game. If both of you have the same temperament and provided there is nothing else going on, you may both agree that it is a wonderful idea and go (and finally taste Jenny's famous sweet and sour pork). If you don't, you might find that one of you is looking forward to the social get together, while the other has their TV tray and latest Netflix show ready to roll, with no intention of meeting poor old Jenny. How would the night end for you as a couple?

OR

You attend a function with your partner on a Wednesday night which ends at 11:30 pm. You get home and end up in bed close to 1 am. You both need to be at work the next day at 8 am. One of you gets up the next day full of energy, having had a luxurious 6.5 hours of sleep while the other wakes up with a major headache, nausea, and feels grumpy for the whole day. How would this impact on future weekdays functions?

> *I remember going on a cruise with my girlfriend and looking forward to all the activities, food, and shows. Because there were only two of us, we ended up being placed at a table with strangers for dinner. To me, this was the best part of the cruise; meeting new mates and just chilling out. But to her, this was horrifying. She didn't say much for the first three nights and only got talking to the other girls on the last night!*
>
> *Guess what? The next cruise was a boys' trip, and so was the one after that!*

Communicate Your Needs to Your Partner

As we will discuss in Chapter 2 and Chapter 3 of this book, being able to articulate your needs is the first step to managing personalities and needs between partners. However, it's important for you to remember that communicating your thoughts and needs does not equate to getting what you want, or even what you need. For example, as much as you might need someone to listen to you as soon as you get home, if your partner needs a winddown time before they can process their thoughts, you may never get the warm welcome you had fancied in your dreams. This is not about telling your partner what you need, but accepting your different personalities and respecting both (even when they mismatch).

Temperament, Compatibility, and Making It Work

As we discussed above, there are traits that you will accept in a lover and others you will not, despite all the willingness in the world. Not everyone will be compatible in relationships. In fact, the saying, "I love them as friends, but could never live with them" illustrates this quite well. It is important to be true to yourself when meeting someone you are considering a long-term relationship with. So yes, love and attention are wonderful, but not enough to sustain a long-term relationship. Consider the differences between commitment, sacrifice, and personality. Consider carefully that even if you and your partner are committed to each other and willing to make sacrifices, there are limits to what we can handle if it goes against your nature. For example, if you are very energetic and insist on going hiking every weekend, at some point, your partner may (or may not) start to resent you and maybe even insist on doing absolutely nothing for the next 25 weekends, behind 12 seasons of their favorite show. If you're an introvert and your partner insists on bringing friends over every Friday nights, you may start feeling anxious about the weekends coming up. To make a long story short, understanding and respecting your partner's needs will go a long way towards a healthy, balanced, and happy relationship.

> *When I met lover boy, I loved how different we were. I was the quiet, shy girl, and he was the popular bad boy. After we moved in together, I wanted him to be more responsible, more focused on the serious stuff. To be more... well, like me. As a loving wife, I did what I thought was right (aren't all wives,*

right?) and tried to turn him into what I needed him to be. Nothing wrong with a 9 to 5 job that pays the bills well. Not surprisingly (well, at the time, I was), we got into major arguments for many years, until I accepted that maybe trying to change him wasn't the answer. In the end, he opened his own little business, super flexible hours and no boss, and guess what? Now, he's both a sexy bad boy AND a family man!

→ CHAPTER 1 TIPS ←

Learn about Your Temperaments. This chapter (like most chapters in this book) is a sample taster of what you have got to look forward to. I invite to read more about the topics if you need to, but for now, this chapter gives you an idea of what temperaments are and will hopefully help you understand how to accept your partner's differences a bit better. Become familiar with the main personality tendencies that you and your partner display, and consider how you will negotiate them rather than try to change them.

Share an Interest. Find a hobby that is new to both of you and interesting to your couple. Whether it is a new TV show, a collection, a physical activity, or simply about the arts, experiencing and discovering something new will give you something to relate together. When partners get to know their other half, particularly in the first five years, they may feel frustrated and annoyed at the unbalance in their temperament. Finding common grounds is extremely helpful in pulling you back together amidst the day-to-day stresses.

Show Interest. Relationships rely on sharing; sharing love, habits, bills, chores, and interests. It is important to have your hobbies and interests, particularly if you have your personality traits but overall, being able to show you care enough to learn about his or her likes and dislikes speaks volume. On top of this, watching someone you love talk, or experience something *they* love can be quite contagious. Worst-case scenario, you get a kick from watching your partner feeling excited, and best-case scenario, you genuinely start liking this activity too.

Don't Fight the Inevitable. There are things that you will not change. You need to accept this right now. Of course, I am not talking about inappropriate behaviors or behaviors that are selfish and damaging to yourself or others. I am talking about genetic dispositions that are inbuilt in you and your partner. Do not think you can or should change your partner's temperament. If they turn into pumpkins past midnight or turn into ice at the mention of something unplanned, the odds are that this will probably be an indication of how well you will need to navigate your unplanned midnight trips from now on. Though, this does not mean you won't be able to negotiate them from time to time, of course.

Do Not Confuse Temperament with Bad Behavior. Once I taught a couple about temperament in therapy. Imagine my surprise when they returned the next week, the husband interpreting my session as permission for not helping with the kids after dinner as he "needed time to wind down when stressed." So, no. Wanting quietness does not mean that you refuse to *ever* let your partner play music, or that needing a good night's sleep means that you let your partner do *all* the baby feeds through the night. Again, no. Regardless of your temperament, loving relationships are about sacrifice and respect. Use common sense to make the distinction.

In Summary

When you meet your special someone, you may be attracted to them for lots of reasons. Some of these may be physical, lifestyle, and even sex. But amongst those, you would be attracted to your partner for the person they are, their personality, ways of dealing with things, and even their little quirks. Then, at some point, those same quirks will drive you crazy and you may find yourself wanting to change the exact thing that you found exciting in the early stages of your relationship. The good news is that this is common, if not normal. The bad news is that it is not going to work, and I advise you to stop. Instead, focus on the differences between personality vs. choices. Personality traits are inbuilt. Choices should be positive and supportive of each other, and should include, at times, compromises. Now that you are on the right track, let's talk about positive communication and the need for concessions in the next couple of chapters.

CHAPTER 1: TRUTH OR DARE

✔ On a piece of paper, write three personality traits of yours and your partner. Then together, discuss. Do you agree with them? Why? Why not?

✔ Write down five activities that you would like to experience on separate pieces of paper. Put both your pieces of paper in a jar. Every week (or as regularly as you can), pick one paper out of the jar and organize the activity. Be genuinely interested and engage in the process. Then share your appreciation with your partner.

✔ On your own, think about what attracted you to your partner in the first place. Has this changed? Why? Why not? What changed about you to alter this perspective?

✔ Sit with your partner and share your first memory of each other. Share the details of how you knew he or she was the "one."

✔ Write down your vision of your partner's perfect day. Go wild and be as dreamy as you wish. Then share the image and see whether you got it right. Once you've discussed this, go on talking about your perfect holiday, house, job, and even kids.

✔ Hide a thank-you note, an appreciation message, or something kind for your partner in their bag, lunchbox, or even under their pillow.

✔ Describe your temperament in three words. Then find three words to describe your partner's. Swap turns and discuss.

Chapter 2

ON COMMUNICATION

Communication in relationships is probably the most vital skill to understand and master: one that I will drum into you through every section of this relationship guide. Without good communication, it is easy to misunderstand your partner and for things to unravel unnecessarily. Picture the following case scenario for a minute. You receive a text from your partner that says, "Don't touch the laundry." How do you interpret it?

> How perfect! I'm granted permission to a chore-free night. What movie should I pick?

> OR

> Bloody hell! Something else I can't do right.

Communication is a mix of sending messages and receiving them, and is always open to interpretation. It is also impacted by the way we feel, the immediate circumstances around us at the time, and history within the relationship. Odds are that if you are in a good mood, having a great day, and are in a good place in your relationship, you will lean towards a positive interpretation of this text. However, the opposite also applies. If you are in a bad mood, just been yelled at by a customer, or had a fight with your partner last night, you may well assume that the text is about having a go at you. A lot of communication issues are about misreading your partner's intention or wishing that your partner could read you like a crystal ball. Either way, communication skills involve the right words, tone, body language, and a willingness to assume the best, rather than automatically assume the worst.

> " *I remember receiving her text that she would cook dinner for our second date. I mean, every other time I would have been keen, but this time, all I could think of was the burnt chicken I made the night before and how she said she was full after one mouthful. But I didn't want to ask her about her motives either. To this day, I still don't know whether she was implying I sucked as a cook or whether she was just returning the favor!*

Let's take time to break down communication into content, tone, and body language. In short, the verbal content in communication relates to the actual words used when exchanging information with your partner. The words chosen to express your thoughts are important. "What do you want?" sounds different to "What could I do for you," though technically it asks the same thing. We tend to use the same type or wording over and over again, and use scripted sentences with set persons. For example, the way we talk to our parent as opposed to a sibling, or the way we talk to our partner as opposed to our neighbor may be very different. Swearing is another good example. I have never heard my adult son swear, though he tells me that apparently if he didn't swear as a chef, he would not get anyone to hear him in the kitchen. Ask yourself, how have my word choices changed over the course of my relationship?

Do I find myself trying less with my partner, or have I noticed that I am more assertive with colleagues than my partner? The answer is probably "yes" because it is human nature, but something to be aware of and address!

When thinking of verbal tone, think of adjectives that could be attached to the words you are using. Descriptions such as aggressive, passive, sad, happy, passionate, interested, threatening, dull, or warm/cold are examples. If your partner said, "I love you" with an aggressive tone, how would you interpret the information? Probably not at face value. Similarly, if your partner said, "I love you" at high volume or high speed, how would you interpret it? Lastly, if they said, "I love you" with a warm tone and a slow-paced speech, how would you then feel about it? Probably pretty darn good compared to the other versions! Our tone is almost more important than what we are saying. If you don't believe me, try speaking to a baby, an animal, or someone who does not speak your language. Say something negative with a very sweet tone, and then try to say something lovely with a cold tone. What happens? This has been done multiple times in studies, and what happens is that the content, though is not understood, is interpreted based on the tone used by the person speaking. So, forget your words for a second, and try to consider your tone when speaking to your partner (and others).

Finally, consider your body language. Do you find yourself staring at your partner when speaking? Making lots of hand movements or invading their personal space? What happens when you smile, gently hold their hand when you address them, or simply look at them when they're asking a question? I bet it is different. Some people have a rowdy and outgoing communication style. They talk with their hands, as my husband would say, and often exude excitement and passion. They may come across as loud but often entertaining as well. Others have a way of expressing themselves that is more reserved, quieter, and does not involve hand signs. They will come across differently in a business meeting even when giving the same presentation. Though there are no right and wrong, it is important to be mindful of your body language and how it speaks to others. Think of examples where your body language might have said a different story and how the mixed messages may have confused your relationship. Body language is as important as your tone and the words you speak.

> "We had decided to watch old home movies from 15 years ago. And so here we were on our honeymoon in Hawaii, having the time of our lives. I recognized our couple, and the husband I have loved for 17 years, but what I didn't recognize was the way he spoke softly to me and the way I waited

'til he was finished speaking to answer him. There definitely was a different tone to our exchanges and the way we danced through our communication.

As I discussed in the introduction, I've decided not to discuss the downfalls of our partners and how they may impact on your relationship, but to focus on the things that we could control in ourselves. However, in this chapter, I highlight how important it is to be able to read your partner's communication skills when it is telling us something essential. For example, what if your partner's body language implied they were frightened during an argument? What if their tone suggested hopelessness or despair, or what if they stopped trying to find words to communicate with you? Those are examples of times where your ability to read your partner is vital. We have a responsibility to acknowledge how we make other people feel and do our best to communicate in a way that is polite, respectful, and safe for both of you. Communication skills are a great tool to manage how we communicate with our partners and to decipher how they might be feeling during exchanges. There are some easy techniques to shape the way we speak to each other. Let's start with two easy ones to master.

"I" messages

Consider those statements.

"You make me feel stupid when you talk about the car," as opposed to "I feel stupid when we talk about the car," or "you always blame me when things go wrong during the holidays," as opposed to "I always feel like I've done something wrong." What do they both imply? How would they both make you and your partner feel in a conversation about the car or the holidays? The odds are that the first sentences would make *your partner* feel like you're blaming them for feeling stupid or being angry at you, while the second would imply that your lack of knowledge about cars make *you* feel stupid or that you are looking for clarification. In short, the first statement may cause your partner to become *defensive* while the second statement may make them feel *protective* of your vulnerable feelings. And yet, as above, in essence, they imply a very similar thing. Consequently, it is important to communicate about our thoughts and feelings using "I" messages, because it can dramatically change people's reaction to what we are trying to say.

"PCiR" model © ("Positive Communication in Relationships")

"I"	"What"	"Why"	"Feedback"

The art of communicating with your partner lay in a very simple method. The components of this formula include using an "I" message, the request, the reason for the request, and feedback from your partner.

It sounds like this in practice:

"I would like you to finish the lawnmowing on Friday so that the yard looks good for little Johnny's birthday party on Saturday. Would that be okay with you?"

OR

"I was hoping to go out with my mom on Sunday to the markets. I could do with a girls' day out. Do you think you'd be okay with that plan?"

> *I must admit, I was a bit sceptical when we left our counseling session with the PCiR hometask sheet. But it worked! It's like my wife could not say no anymore to my fishing trips when I put it like that. Okay, not quite a magical wand, but close to it!*

My husband has often commented that communicating with partners shouldn't be that much work. However, the reality is that 90% of the couples I see in therapy attend my rooms for communication issues that could be resolved quickly if they only practiced those simple exercises. If we were to pull the PCiR apart, we would observe all the important components that make it work well. Firstly, the "I" message takes away any blame and focuses the request back on to the facts, rather than emotions. Second, the "what" adds content that is clear, concise, and factual. It takes away any subjective meaning that may exist, or that may distract from the information. Thirdly, the "why" focuses on the reason, which may assist in making sense of the request. For example, if your partner asked not to do the dishes, though it's their turn, due to having to finish an urgent presentation, as opposed to just wanting to catch up on live sports, you may be more inclined to take over their boring duty in a bid to be supportive. Finally, adding feedback is a way to be polite, show respect, and shape the whole question as a request, rather than a non-negotiable statement.

Communicating in a polite, non-blaming, respectful, and positive manner is the key to a successful relationship, and if you have the tools, you should try to use them. However, there are times where even with good communication, it can be challenging to communicate with your partner. Let's have a look at some issues and simple tips.

→ Chapter 2 Tips ←

Poor Timing. Who has not attempted to speak to their partner, only to realize the timing was pretty poor? Things like starting a serious conversation when your partner is on the toilet, watching an episode of their favorite TV show, or simply half asleep isn't a bright idea. You need to ensure that you choose an appropriate timing if you need to discuss an important topic. This might include a time where you are both rested, calm, fed, and ready to talk.

Enough Time. You may have decided to start talking to your partner about something really important while waiting for a visit from your mother. Surely you learned that this was a mistake. Do not start an emotional conversation if you have a limited timeframe. Thirty minutes, or even an hour, is not enough to discuss your decision to get a vasectomy or to let your partner know that you're thinking of moving to another state. Allow enough time to prep for your topic, discuss the matter, and wrap up both your thoughts and feelings before being interrupted by something else.

Location, Location, Location. Have you considered the impact of *where* you will be talking to your partner about important things? Is the bathroom, the kids' playroom, or on the train, the best place to be talking about private and emotional things? Where do you feel safe and comfortable? What about your partner? Where are you likely to have *enough* of the *right* time? For some, it might be their bedrooms. For others, it might be on a nice walk down the beach. It doesn't matter, as long as it is a safe place for both of you and gives you the privacy and the time to express your thoughts and feelings about a particular topic.

Actively Listen. This means exactly that. Our brains are not wired to talk and listen at the same time. Therefore, we can only prioritize one. Unfortunately, a lot of couples seeking my help have focused on the wrong one. If you are busy talking over your partner's voice, you cannot physically listen and hear what they have to say. If you Google "active listening," you will find a great deal of good information on how to master the art of listening in a way that allows you to show your partner interest and confirm that you heard them. In short, this may include the use of silence when appropriate, making completely sure your partner has finished speaking before answering and being aware of your tone, body language, and word choice. First and foremost, if you find yourself thinking about what you will say next *while* your partner is talking, you are *not* listening to them.

Heart-Rate Test. When talking about important things, we may find ourselves getting worked up and emotional. This impacts on our ability to communicate and get messages across. Further, it sometimes means that we may say things we regret or do not mean. We may notice an increase in gesturing, increase in speech volume, or a difference in our tone. When this happens, a quick check-in revolves in measuring our heart rate for fifteen seconds. A heart rate of over 25 beats per 15 seconds means that you are no longer in a space to be processing the conversation with your partner as constructively as you could. If this is the case, take a break until your heart rate (beats per 15 seconds) measures under 18. This will allow you to communicate calmly and proactively without your brain shutting down.

The Habit of Sharing. Imagine that the only time you spoke to your partner was about bills, children, or emergencies. You would quickly start associating your interactions with problems, resentment, anxiety, or negativity. For people to talk well together, they have to talk altogether. This means practicing talking when things are well, funny, emotional, stressful, serious, and everything in between. It means listening, taking turns, not interrupting, and showing interest in your partner's Marvel movies, latest work gossip, or choice of wardrobe, because it is much easier to feel comfortable speaking to your partner when you speak together on a regular basis than it is to broach a difficult conversation with no practice in reading your partner's body language, reactions, or overall mood. So, make a point to "chat" everyday about work, study, family, or current affairs in a way that is enjoyable and light-hearted. This will make a difference when you need to speak about serious issues.

In Summary

Communication skills are the most important to develop and maintain over the course of your relationship. Those will be the skills that dictate whether you resolve arguments, show interest in your partner's likes and dislikes, can express your thoughts and feelings, and move towards the same direction in the future. As I stated earlier, the majority of couples I see in therapy love each other but have forgotten the basics of communication. We will expand on this in the next couple of chapters, but in the meantime, remember that simple, open, and positive communication is the key to a successful relationship.

CHAPTER 2: TRUTH OR DARE

✔ Ask your partner about their day and listen without interrupting. Practice asking questions, allow them to finish without jumping in, and show with your body language that you are interested. At the end, discuss how your partner felt about the conversation.

✔ Using the PCiR model, ask your partner for a favor. First, ask the way you would normally ask, and second, ask using the PCiR model. See whether it makes a difference and assess your partner's response about the favor.

✔ Record* a conversation between you and your partner for 15 minutes. Listen to it and note your tone, choice of words, use of silence, or whether you are talking over them. Consider how you could have the conversation differently.

✔ Watch a video where both you and your partner feature. Observe your body language, your eye contact, simple, affectionate gestures, or interactions with a third party. Consider and discuss with your partner what you're noticing, liking, or disliking about your observations.

✔ Commit to speaking to each other as if your manager/ mother/someone of your choice was in the room.

✔ Measure your heart rate during a conversation. If heart rate is above 25 beats/15 seconds, take a break and wait until your heartbeat is under 18 beats/15 seconds. Note whether this is helpful.

✔ Express your thanks to your partner for the simple things and always use manners and consideration, particularly for things they do routinely.

*It is illegal to record someone without their knowledge to use that information against them. Get your partner's permission to record one conversation before you do it. They do not need to know which conversation it will be but will need to be aware of the purpose of it.

MEETING
IN THE MIDDLE

As you embark on your relationship and outgrow the honeymoon period, you may find yourself arguing with your partner about decisions, thoughts, and behaviors. Some of those arguments will be about substantial issues, while others will be about the small things. Do not fear. It's normal. I have yet to meet a couple who does not have disputes over routine choices and who manages to negotiate without an adjustment period.

> *We had been living together for six days! Six days! And he rocks up with five mates, at 10 pm, and enough alcohol to last him three months. How was I supposed to negotiate this in advance? I never even imagined anyone would think this was okay!*
>
> *Okay. Maybe screaming through the door that I just found his lost script for Viagra wasn't the most assertive way to handle it, but to this day, he now gives me warning!*

The importance of negotiating comes close second after the art of learning to communicate in relationships. Couples negotiate together throughout their whole lives, and while there are topics we cannot compromise (we will discuss this below), our approach and reaction to those topics should be able to be discussed and settled in healthy relationships.

All of us are born and raised in different ways. We come complete with trauma, baggage, culture, history, likes and dislikes, values, attitudes, and spiritual beliefs. Some of those things are quite deep and personal. Some of those things cannot be changed, and we should accept them as part of our partner's identity, to a degree. If we don't understand those factors in our partnership, they can cause friction at some point. Let's take religion as an example. It is common for partners of different faiths to be in a relationship. This is not a problem as long as both partners are respectful of each other's' beliefs, and can agree to discuss new variables as they come. Let's take a couple, for example, who have been together for five years and attend their different churches in peace. Five years later, children come along, and one of the partners expects that the children will follow his/her religion. Is this okay? Why? Why not?

It's easy to see how a couple's own religious beliefs should not have to be negotiated. What about the faith that their children will belong to? What happens if this is not negotiated well before the children come along? False assumptions like having a "superior" religion, or being of a specific gender or age, do not mean that children should automatically be raised in one faith at the expense of the other, *without* having negotiated this appropriately. Distinguish between core values that properly belong to us and the need to negotiate how those same core values impact on our relationship, personal wellbeing, and family life.

On Becoming Assertive

First things first. Couples cannot successfully meet in the middle unless they can learn to be assertive through this process. There are three main ways to negotiate: aggressively, passively, and assertively, though many of us have been known to mix and match using the passive-aggressive method.

1. Aggressive Approach

When a partner is aggressive, they often use a tone that is unpleasant/threatening/sharp, accompanied by a similar body language (revisit Chapter 1, if needed). When negotiating, partners who show an aggressive approach often come into the negotiation with their agenda, a lack of flexibility, their minds made up, and a core belief that their needs come before the needs of their partners. In those cases, negotiation often ends with the aggressive partner "winning" and the other partner feeling resentful and disempowered. This is generally not conducive to a good and healthy relationship.

2. Passive Approach

Partners who show a passive approach generally give in to their partner, in a way that is too easy and lacks depth and discussion. They often feel upset at themselves afterward and a decline in communication generally occurs in those relationships. This is because the passive person starts to wonder "what's the point?" and because their partner quickly realizes that there is little input coming from the passive person, therefore, indeed, "what's the point?" This can lead to feeling helpless in our relationship and ourselves.

3. Assertive Approach

This approach is most effective. It considers that both partners are equal and comfortable sharing their point of view in a way that respects each other's needs, thoughts, and feelings. In assertive negotiations, both members show interest in the issue, consider all the options, and explain why they agree or disagree. Couples who can communicate and negotiate assertively are more likely to be happy with the outcome of their common decision and stick to it. They're also less likely to have relationship issues across time.

Aggressive	Passive	Assertive
Overpowering approach	Disempowered approach	Balanced approach
Own needs first	Own needs last	Both needs considered
Will intimidate partner	Will frustrate partner	Fosters healthy relationship

On the Nitty-Gritty of Negotiation Skills

For a while, as I trained as a clinical social worker, I wrongly assumed that people learned communication skills at school, at home, at kids' clubs, or similar. Imagine my surprise when I realized that I would have work guaranteed until post-retirement, because these days, communication and negotiation basics are not routinely taught. Realistically, as awesome as modern living is, our fast-paced lifestyles have impacted our ability to communicate. So, how do we apply the nitty-gritty of negotiation skills? We've established that being assertive is compulsory. What comes next? Here are some guidelines to get you ready to meet your partner in the middle.

Are You Prepared to Compromise?

Before you can negotiate assertively (remember that *assertively* is the keyword is), you need to prepare for this conversation. That includes meeting your partner with the right attitude, body language, and tone, *I messages*, and a genuinely open mind. You also need to set up this meeting at the right moment, and in the right location, to ensure that you can speak without getting disturbed for as long as it is required.

Before you begin negotiation, you both need to know what you're negotiating for. What is the issue? How is it a problem? How do you foresee things unraveling if you don't do anything about it?

> I texted my husband that we needed to have a family meeting about a problem we were having. He came in looking puzzled about what the fuss was about. I braced myself for any attempts at manipulation and my tone made sure he knew that. After 10 minutes, though, he asked "what are we actually talking about?" I answered and he laughed! But not with a sarcastic laugh, rather, an innocent laugh, really. Then he said, "baby, I wish I had known this was a problem for you!" It turned out he simply didn't know how I felt, and as soon as he did, he agreed to change the way we banked.

Once you have worked out that there is an issue, and have agreed to discuss it, you may want to process a couple of preliminary thoughts individually before you meet. Some of those may include:

- ✔ What is it that I would like to happen?
- ✔ Why? Relevance and importance?
- ✔ What is negotiable and not negotiable in this discussion?
- ✔ Why is the topic important/difficult/sensitive to my partner?
- ✔ How do I feel about my partner's needs on this topic?
- ✔ What am I prepared to compromise/sacrifice to negotiate this in my favor?

It is important to come in prepared, but those questions are only the beginning. Let's have a look at starting the discussion now.

Starting the Discussion

You will need to start your discussion with a clear idea of what the issue is and why. It is important to use *I messages,* and focus on objective information initially (do not start with emotions, thoughts, and feelings. Start with the facts).

This may sound like something like this.

> "We seem to disagree on whether we need to invest in this new investment property. There are pros and cons, and I think it would be good to discuss them all so we can agree on where to go from here."

You can see how this is inviting and non-threatening, as opposed to something like this.

> "As usual, you can't agree with common sense, so here's to another two hours of headache-inducing waffling."

By the way, if any of you thought the second example was anything *but* a terrible and shameful response, you need to book a time to see me to clarify the basics again.

In all seriousness, you or your partner's opening statement gives both of you the chance to name the issue and depersonalize it, leading to sharing your thoughts respectfully on the topic. It is a great place to start.

Sharing Points of View

Remember the PCiR model from Chapter 1? It will come in handy here. Once you have come to the discussion, prepared in body and mind, and can clearly articulate what the issue is, both partners can share their point of views. This includes the right wording, tone, and body language. (I was not kidding in Chapter 1 when I said communication was going to be drummed into you throughout this book.) Sharing points of view revolves around the flow of ideas, back and forth, in a way that fosters a discussion around the topic at hand. Raising the issue objectively, having the opportunity to listen, and visualizing opportunities and consequences are important. In very short, this is about:

- ✔ **Taking turns** – Each partner should take turns at speaking about the issue and the impact it has on them. During this time, it is important to listen actively and not interrupt.

- ✔ **Brainstorming** – Both partners should be comfortable to present potential solutions, describe them, and explain how and why they chose them.

- ✔ **Responding** – The partner who listened to the option/ solution should reply with their thoughts, opinions, and considerations.

This step needs to occur respectfully and as patiently as you can. Never lose sight that you are batting on the same team!

On the Actual Craft of the "Back and Forth"

So, imagine the negotiations that need to occur when buying a car. You walk in a car yard with a plan to spend ten thousand dollars, but find the perfect car for twelve thousand. Neither you nor the salesman is prepared to give in. What happens then? Slowly, the salesman starts pitching in and offers you very slow bargaining chips. It might be free car seats, or it might be a full tank of gas. You reply by telling him that you came here with eight thousand, and you will not spend a dollar more. So, the salesman goes and checks with his boss (something that's probably designed to get us hopeful) and returns with a great offer of eleven thousand dollars for the car, last offer; take it or leave it. By then, you probably tell him it is so sad, but that you really can only afford as far as nine thousand and prepare to walk away, as slowly as it takes for the salesman to wing his next offer. You step one foot behind the car yard threshold when the salesman yells out that if *only* you were willing to go to ten thousand, he would be able to get you not only the car, but also those car seats and a full tank of gas. You then turn around and shake hands. Him, thinking he made a great sale, and you, knowing that you planned on spending 10,000 all along. Happy days!

Though I would not dare compare relationship negotiations with the sales of cars, I'd like to point out some similarities respectfully. Firstly, both persons wanted something in that exchange. Both hoped for a good outcome that suited their own needs, both carefully considered what they were prepared to offer/not offer, and both were willing to go back and forth until they got to where they needed to go.

Negotiations are about going back and forth with offers, suggestions, and alternatives, until both parties are happy, or at least content with the proposal. It's about agreeing to a compromise; a middle where things won't be 100% like you hoped they'd be, but still acceptable to your standards. It's about both of you winning the argument and not one of you winning at the expense of the other. Although in a relationship, a partner might completely give up an argument in view of being granted a win in a different argument. That works too.

$\longrightarrow$ **Chapter 3 Tips** $\longleftarrow$

"I messages." Did we talk about "I messages" yet? I cannot repeat this enough. You should not speak on behalf of your partner. You should speak about how *you* feel, and this very simple method will truly impact on how your loved one receives your message. Make a point to speak with "I" and to describe facts and reasons rather than subjective or blaming statements. Remember to use the PCiR model and treat your spouse like you would strangers or work colleagues, so basically, with clear respect free from emotional overload.

Open-Ended Questions. Pay attention to your line of questioning. Closed questions (questions that require a yes/no answer) often limit the quality of discussions. For example, imagine if your partner asked you, "do you want to sort [name of issue] out?" What would you automatically answer? Yes/no/what do you think? In comparison, open-ended questions (questions that start with what/why/how/where, etc.) generally assist in generating thinking. Using the same example, how would you answer your partner if they asked you "What were you hoping to see happen with [name of issue]?" You would most likely answer with some form of descriptive or explanation. Clearly, open-ended questions invite for more reflection, and I would encourage to use those when appropriate (Disclaimer: Yes, there are times where yes/no is preferable. I know, I know. It's confusing, but we will talk about this later).

Choose Your Battles. Couples go through multiple debates over the course of their relationship. It's not possible to win them all, nor do you want to negotiate every single thing that bothers you. In healthy relationships, partners will take turns at supporting their loved one with things that are important to them (even if you don't agree with them). Filter the important from the trivial, and select what is worth arguing about. In a sense, imagine that there is a set number of battles you can win. Would you want to win a silly battle, or would you prefer to save your energy for a battle that you take to heart? To say it casually, don't sweat the small stuff if you don't have to.

Nurture Your Relationship. It is important to remember that both you and your partner are on the same side. Never lose track of this fact, even when you are arguing for opposite causes. To meet in the middle, it might be useful to consider the positive aspects of your partner, their efforts, the quality of your relationship, and what made you fall in love in the first place. It is also important to take the time to be friends, go on dates, and have fun. It is much easier to negotiate with someone when you feel kind and tender towards them than when we feel angry or resentful.

In Summary

As highlighted in Chapter 2, communication skills, whether through discussions or negotiations, is paramount. It is the most important set of skills to have for couples wanting to stay together for the long haul (though, let's not kid ourselves, it is also powerful for couples who do not stay together). Having differences of opinion in your relationship is not a reflection of having a good or bad relationship; it is a reflection of being human. The key is in being able to navigate those disagreements in a clear, respectful, practical, and proactive manner. I promise you that if you strive to keep open communication channels with your partner, drop the routine assumptions, and develop a willingness to meet your partner in the middle, you are halfway there.

CHAPTER 3: TRUTH OR DARE

✔ Write a list of things you feel are values based and therefore non-negotiable. Then write a list of the things you feel should be negotiable, even if you do not like your partner's viewpoint on it. Find a way to make the distinction between the negotiable vs. non-negotiable topics. More importantly, you need to open your mind to the fact that there should be a limited number of non-negotiables compared to what you should be prepared to discuss across the lifespan of your relationship.

✔ Write a list of appropriate times and places to have an important discussion with your partner. Then write a list of inappropriate times and places for your couple. Reflect on your rationale, and discuss with your partner.

✔ Pick any topic (it does not have to be a contentious issue) and practice asking five close-ended question, and then five open-ended questions each about the subject. Discuss the differences and how it helped/did not help with the flow of the conversation.

✔ Choose a topic and an opening statement, and practice saying it with an aggressive, then passive, and finally, an assertive tone and body language. Make it fun and discuss your findings as a couple. You could even video yourself for more live entertainment.

✔ Pick a small issue to discuss with your partner and reverse your roles. Imagine your partner's point of view, his or her thoughts and feelings about the issue, and argue in favor of their perspective. This will help in both of you developing empathy in the argument and visualizing potential compromises.

✔ Ask to discuss a small issue with your partner using an opening statement and applying the PCiR model (*I message,* name the issue, state why it is a problem, and invite them to reflect on alternatives).

✔ Pick a real bone of contention and practice all those steps, including the back and forth until you both agree to meet in the middle. Compare this with previous attempts at negotiating together.

PART TWO

A Small Couple in a Big World

SHARING DREAMS, GOALS, AND VALUES

Think about dreams, goals, and values for a second. Ask yourself whether these make your relationship work better, or make your relationship rocky. Try to remember what your dreams and goals were when you were single, and then when you became a couple. How have they strengthened or changed since then?

When you consider your relationship goals, consider the direction of these goals. In short, which way are your goals, dreams, or values directing you towards? Or is it that you see no direction in the way you or your relationship is going? Without direction, we tend to pause, wait around, or even feel like we are going around in circles. Imagine you and your partner are on a boat, going nowhere. How safe would you feel? How excited would you feel about the future? The odds are that each day would start to look the same, and you may wonder about life's purpose, even.

What I noticed in working with couples over the years, is that holding compatible goals is as important as having goals altogether. The partners I have seen in therapy who have no goals or dreams often become stagnant, both in themselves and in the relationship.

Without a driving force or a motion towards something, people stop moving and so does their relationship. I have a favorite story that I like to tell my therapy clients, and it is beautifully written by Viktor Frankl in *Man's Search for Meaning.* In his book, Frankl explains that human beings need a purpose to live, and without it, they first start to die spiritually, then physically give up; a phenomenon he observed during the war (I highly recommend his book, by the way). While for a minority of us, goals and purpose are not linked, the truth is that goals and dreams are often building blocks towards a bigger end. For example, studying towards a job we want may indeed be about getting a stable and good income, but for what aim? It may be to provide for our family, to discover the world, or simply because that particular profession makes us feel powerful or useful. In any case, the decision of which profession to hold impacts on our bigger role, the same way our values impact our decisions, goals, and purpose we give to our lives. Therefore, we need to be aware of our values, dreams, ambitions, and how those fit with ourselves and within our couple.

> I remember our first counselling session, where Dr. Azri asked us about our goals. We both had so much to say! I went on about how I wanted to open our own business and would need to work hard for at least a decade. No holidays, no wild spending, and seven days a week working and building up our restaurant. Then it was my partner's turn, and he said he wanted to commit to visiting his parents in Italy at least once a year and sending monthly allowances to help them in their retirement!
>
> A restaurant in Italy, maybe?

It is healthy and beneficial for couples to establish relationship goals. For some, it is a very formal process where they meet and negotiate plans, while for others, it is an implied process of simultaneous navigation towards something they both are attracted to. For example, getting married, having children, a particular balance between business and pleasure, or achieving particular steps as they progress as individuals and as a couple. For example, imagine the couple whose wife feels strongly about staying home after having children (until they are at least out of high school) with a husband who believes in wealth building and professional career development through the lifespan. Or the couple with one partner who dreams of climbing Mt. Everest, in a relationship with someone who openly admits to hating the outdoors and traveling. You get my gist. Dreams, goals, and values are unique and personal. However, couples should also have their dreams, goals, and values to keep them moving forward. These may not need to be completely the same, but they should be somewhat compatible or workable in your couple.

I want to remind you that this is NOT about forgetting who you are and what you want for yourself. Creating common goals can only be done successfully when you have common things to work with. If partners have very different views of work, holidays, parenting, religion, etc., as well as their general purpose, they may struggle coming up with common dreams. That is okay. Sharing dreams and goals is not a chore. It is a privilege that should excite us, so enjoy the discovery as well. Remember how I promised you that communication skills would be the most important topic in this book? I was not lying. This applies here too. Couples who have very different outlooks on life can still share dreams and goals. It is about listening to our partner's visions and imagining them in context. When we love and respect someone else, we become interested in what they care about and naturally, and it grows on us too. And if this fails, you do not have to enjoy or share your partner's dream to accept that *they are excited by it.*

> *Would someone explain to me how an introverted academic became a Marvel expert after a couple of decades of being married to a geek?*
>
> *Wolverine, Spiderman, Green Goblin, Captain America, Hulk, Iron Fist, Daredevil, Deadpool, Luke Cage... But of course, no one beats team Iron Man!*

What if Couples Have Very Different Goals and Dreams?

Couples often ask this question, and I still find it difficult to answer it. The truth is that the less common points you have with your partner, including different goals, dreams, and values, the harder the relationship can be to manage. For many, what happens is that one of the partners gets their way, while the other one adjusts to new goals and dreams. This may be the stay-at-home wishful parent who agrees to go back to work or the hopeful homeowner who ends up renting across the country as they travel for the next decade. For many, it is about compromise (nothing wrong with that); letting go of some relationship dreams for the benefit of other goals. While very different dreams and values can strain a relationship, it does not mean that couples with different goals are doomed. These relationships are as good as how much the partners are willing to work on their communication skills and their willingness to compromise.

If you have very different goals in your relationship, ask yourself; is this about power? Is this about incompatible differences, or is this about taking the time to learn about your partner's dreams and showing interest? Most couples can find some common ground if they try hard enough. However, if you are in the very early stages of your relationship, and genuinely cannot see any common values or goals, I would suggest you consider whether this is something that would change with time or a reflection of a poorly matched partnership. I do not have the answer, clearly, and I can only encourage you to learn about the importance of finding common grounds and the need to apply good negotiation skills with your loved one to ensure that this works well for both of you.

Why Set Goals?

1. **Goals and dreams give us purpose.** Without purpose, we are as good as dead. (Seriously. Ask Victor Frankl.)

2. **Goals and dreams help relationships move forward and grow together towards a common objective.**

3. **Setting up goals together require good communication skills and appreciation of each other.** It is good practice and gives us the opportunity to share about ourselves and our visions.

4. **Dreams keep us going when the going gets tough.** They provide us with something to look forward to through life.

5. **When we do achieve these goals and dreams, we feel awesome.** It gives couples a reason to celebrate achievements and strengthen relationships.

What Kind of Relationship Goals?

You can pick any areas for yourself and your couple. These may be professional, about relationships skills or development, financial, parenting, about hobbies or interests, about in-laws and friends, or about chores in general. Remember that sharing dreams and goals is as much about respect, a willingness to compromise, and about understanding your partner's values as it is about the goals themselves. It is about seeking a forward movement to assist your relationship in progressing towards more exciting things. And what is exciting for one couple, may not be for another, so it is really about what makes your relationship tick.

$\rightarrow$ Chapter 4 Tips $\leftarrow$

Start the conversation. Pick a topic and start sharing your thoughts on it. Is this a topic that you both agree should be a goal for your relationship? Is this something that would be nice (i.e., financial stability) or something that needs to happen (i.e., working on communication skills or appreciation of each other)? Share your thoughts, your excitement, and your fears about setting goals. Be honest and patient towards each other.

Write a List. Write a list of short-term, medium-term, and long-term goals. Separate them into their categories and consider how important they are to you (from non-negotiable to "meh"). How do you feel about all your goals? Can you clearly articulate the short-term, with the long-term, versus your own goals with your relationship dreams? Practice describing them and their importance to a friend. If they are not clear, make them clearer.

Prioritize. There is no way that all couples will ever achieve, or even agree on all their goals. It is important to prioritize the visions that you feel would need to exist in your life to make you feel fulfilled, with the ones that are more average. Can you see the ones that reflect your values with the ones that are more practical, for instance? Can you see the ones that you could remove from your list as opposed to the ones you feel are a priority?

Communicate. If I have not said this enough already, let me say it again. The only doomed couples are couples who refuse to communicate positively. With good negotiation, communication, and empathy, both partners can feel listened to, fulfilled, and happy in their lives. It is not always easy to agree on very different topics, but if you respect your partner's point of view, you most always will always find a way to meet in the middle (and if you do not, make a time to see me).

SMART. This cool acronym stands for "Smart, Measurable, Achievable, Realistic, and Timely." When you set up a goal, how do you make sure it meets the SMART rule? Is it an important goal? How will you measure its success? Is this something you can achieve? For instance, you may want to get married on the moon, but the odds are that it is not very achievable or realistic in today's era. Finally, what kind of timeframe are you giving your goal? Timeframes can be revisited, but they give us good guidelines. By following the SMART acronym, you will develop goals and dreams that are more likely to succeed.

Be Flexible. Sometimes our situations change over time. Sometimes it is a good thing, but regardless, it means that some of our goals may not matter anymore or simply feel different. Be flexible with yourself and with your relationship goals. If you had a dream to buy your dream home by the beach, but you both got a job in the city, it might make more sense to buy in the city for the time being. It does not mean that you gave up on your dream, but that you adapted to a different dream, based on a change of circumstances.

Celebrate. All of your achievements. The small ones, yours, your partner's, and your couple's. Write them down, cross them out, have a party, scream it on the rooftop; it does not matter, as long as you give yourselves the opportunity to celebrate the goals and dreams that you managed to complete. These will give you the motivation to create new goals, inject you with the energy to work on your new projects and make you feel good.

In Summary

Sharing common goals in relationships help solidify the direction in which the couple is going. It gives partners mutual ground and a focus to work towards a healthy, happy, and positive relationships. It is easier when partners have similar interests, values, and dreams. However, if you do not, do not panic. The key lies in communication and in the couple's willingness to compromise and negotiate that direction. Think of goals and dreams as building blocks of all shapes and sizes, making up your great, fun, and loving relationship pathway to happiness. Some of these blocks are small and are easy. Others are huge and feel like a massive accomplishment when finished. We, as individuals, have our dreams. Things we always wanted to realize, and things that matter to us. It is the same for couples. Couples have their path, leading to a place that represents what is important to them. I wish for you to find that place, and have great fun in the process!

CHAPTER 4: TRUTH OR DARE

✔ Write a mission statement about your life as individuals, and then as a couple. What are your priorities, your values, and, in essence, what is important to you?

✔ Make up a vision board. Use magazine photos, print quotes or messages, or draw or write about your dreams and goals. Then place the vision board somewhere you can see it, so it can inspire and motivate you.

✔ Write a list of goals and dreams, and highlight the important ones. Make a note of why you chose them and why you left some out. Define those you would be willing to let go and those you truly care about.

✔ Ask your partner about their bigger personal goal. Ask lots of question and genuinely show interest. Then reflect on whether you are surprised or not.

✔ As a couple, write down five relationship goals. Then score them from the most important (1) to the least important (5). Then use the SMART rule to talk about how you could achieve them.

✔ Write a letter to yourself to open in five years' time. Describe who you are, where you are living, your job, achievements, and dreams. Share your pride, worries, and what you hope your life will be with your partner in five years' time. Five years later, read it, and ponder on what went well, not so well, and why.

 ✔ Similar to the challenge above, imagine you are five years older and run into an old school friend. Imagine you are telling him/her all about your future life. How would you imagine it? What goals and dreams would you have achieved and how?

DEALING WITH FRIENDS AND FAMILY

T he next step in all relationships is to extend the bubble of love from your little couple to include others like friends and family. Welcome, Uncle John, Cousin Sylvia, best friend Harry, and BFF Jenny, to the circle of love!

Is That Silence I Hear?

Okay, yes. This is a loaded chapter. For many, it is awesome to add some extra fun and love to the relationship. However, for others, it brings complications and frustrations, and to a degree, you will need to apply everything we have learned so far to these new extended relationships. So, let's get started on another fun journey in *The REAL Guide to Life as a Couple.*

Generally speaking, unless you have met through friends or relatives, you will probably meet your in-laws or partner's friends once you are established as a somewhat serious couple. These encounters are often daunting for the new person and might even turn out to be a ground for judging, permission seeking, or last tick of approval before your new relationship's big step. In the movies, we might see the new in-laws being super warm and friendly, and friends being completely accepting; or it could be the complete opposite. The likes of *Meet the Fockers* or *Everybody Loves Raymond* portray more difficult bonding, with in-laws and friends bringing their own set of troubles to the relationships. (I suggest that if your soon-to-be father-in-law insists on taking you to a basement to bind you in some way, shape, or form, RUN.)

Meeting your partner's relatives and friends is full on. No matter how we put it, there is pressure to get along with them, be accepted by them, and all fit in as a happy family. However, the reality is somewhat in the middle. Most of these meetings are neutral, initially, and relationships may take time to develop. Like with any relationships, you all may feel like you need to be on your best behavior initially, but with time, you will start to be yourselves and discuss your thoughts, values, and opinions. The same may apply to your own family. This is where things go well or go sour.

> *My boyfriend invited me to his family's home for Thanksgiving. I was as much excited as I was nervous! His mom opened the door and hugged me, like she had known me all her life while his three sisters all sat across me, grilling me with a hundred questions! One of them even wrote notes!*
>
> *To this day, I reckon this first meeting was worse to any job interview I have ever gone to!*

Some of the signs that things are not going as well as you both hoped with your extended relationships might be:

- ✔ Avoidance of family/social events (where you might come up with every excuse under the sun to avoid seeing the in-laws, friends, and your own family)

- ✔ Arguing over friends or relatives (if the mention of their names leads to an argument, you're probably in the running)

- ✔ Breakdown in communication between you and your partner (shutting down as the result of feeling hurt/frustrated/torn, etc.)

- ✔ Relationship issues over random things (Snowball effect; once it starts, it starts)

- ✔ Open arguments with the in-laws/friends when you do see them that do not resolve (sort of a good clue)

- ✔ Your family/friends openly rejecting your partner (not inviting them to Christmas, birthdays, or family events is also a very good clue)

- ✔ Physical threats or fights (clearly if you get to this, you need to stop seeing them and possibly involve the police or a neutral party)

How Do I Work with My Partner with our Family and Friends?

What we know is that even in the best world of families, issues come up. They might be big or small and may resolve quickly, but may cause frustration in your relationship nonetheless. Because this book is about your relationship with your partner, let's now focus on how you should manage any potential tension, conflict, rules, or uncertainties about family and friends in your relationship.

First, it is important to accept that friends and family are important for most people. It is sad and tricky to have to pick between two people we love, and generally, this notion of "picking" doesn't end well for any parties. It is smart to accept that for your partner, his/her friends and family are significant. Every time he or she may feel trapped in the middle, they may grow resentful towards the situation, in a non-constructive way (this is where Chapter 2 comes in handy. Revisit assertive communication if you need the refresher). In the end, an improved relationship between friends/family and yourselves will create relationship harmony.

The key to working out issues with friends and family is to remember who the priority is. In this case, the priority is your relationship; you and your partner. This means that in principle (and provided you and your partner are reasonable with your demands and decisions), you need to be together with your partner against conflicts that may arise. It truly important for partners to feel that they are the priority in their lover's life; that they have each other's backs if it comes to it. However, you need to agree on what the issues are, agree on options to resolve them, communicate in an assertive and respectful way, not to take the conflict personally, and negotiate (Go on. Go back to Chapters 2 and 3).

> " The hardest step for my girlfriend and I was to agree on boundaries when it came to her sister rocking up in the middle of the night after a night out (we lived in the city, not far from her favorite club).
>
> My girlfriend was raised super strictly and I am pretty easy going. Therefore, our "consequences" went from military action to a slight tap on the wrist! In the end, I gladly let them sort it out between themselves directly.
>
> Three females arguing in the same flat was too much for me to handle!

If there are issues with your partner's friends or family, acknowledge these. Set clear boundaries and limits. As I tell all my clients in therapy, there are three steps to healthy boundaries. The first one is about deciding what the boundary should be. Is it okay for your mother-in-law to give soft drinks to your children every time they come over? What about lending money to friends? Once you have decided what is okay with you, and what is not, you will be in a better position to let people know.

This brings us to the second step. Part 2 of good boundaries is to let everyone know about them. There is no point in deciding that soft drinks are banned in your children's stomach if you don't intend to let Grandma know. Unless she has a crystal ball, she is not going to know and will probably stock up her fridge with Fanta at every family gathering. Now, these two steps are common sense and most of us have no trouble applying them. The third step is a little trickier, but like I say to my therapy clients, a boundary without Step Three is no boundary.

Now, the thing about boundaries is that they are subjective and individual. I might feel that a good boundary for my family is "text before showing up," to ensure I am home and dressed, while for someone else, this may be silly and unnecessary. The same applies to natural consequences. I might feel that a particular consequence is appropriate while another person may decide on a completely different one. There is no right or wrong, as long as these are clear, respectful, and obviously safe and legal.

Step Three is about protecting your boundary. What are you prepared to do to ensure that people take you seriously and respect your wish? How will you follow through? In line with our example, if Grandma continues to offer Fanta to your children on every occasion, despite knowing your rule, what will you do? Step Three is about setting up a natural consequence. This does not mean revenge, a punishment, or something vindictive. No, it means that you have clearly explained your boundary, and highlighted what would need to occur if the behavior continued. This means that if Grandma continues dishing out soft drinks for little Jimmy, you may decide that little Jimmy would not stay at Grandma's without supervision, that Grandma needs to visit little Jimmy at your house or the park, or that Grandma will not see Little Jimmy until she understands that soft drinks are not allowed for whatever reason. Step Three is hard because it may involve conflict and confrontation. But without it, you have not set out a clear and constructive boundary.

The way Dr. Azri taught me about boundaries was by pretending she wanted to kick me and making me go through all the steps that would need to happen for her to stop! It was so weird and funny, and yet, such a practical and visual way to work out the importance of the three steps to a boundary.

To this day, I have never forgotten!

Being honest is another central factor in managing friends and relatives. Do not tell your partner or his/her friends that everything is fine if it is not. What do you think will happen over time? You will only become upset, passive-aggressive, or withdrawn. Be honest and speak the truth, and do not involve a third party in relaying any information. For example, if Aunty Jenny upsets you by saying that your casserole was terrible in public at the last family dinner, ask to speak to Aunty Jenny alone, then directly and calmly explain how you feel and why. By not putting your partner in the middle, you are giving your partner and yourself the chance to build relationships and healthy communication with the other parties, and simply saving on tension and arguments later.

What if There are Some Real Issues with our Friends or Family?

Unfortunately, at times, good communication and boundaries are not enough to fix a very poor relationship between two people. Sometimes, it involves tension, pressure, and negativity. It is important that you and your partner are clear on how to manage this and stick together.

✓ **Stand your ground.** As the old saying goes, if you give in an inch, you'll be asked to give a mile. Set boundaries and rules as a couple and stick to them. This does not mean that you cannot negotiate or simply change your mind, but it might mean that what was important at some point, no longer is. There is a difference in moving your boundary because you choose to, as opposed to feeling coerced.

✔ **Remember that you are entitled to being an expert in your life and your choices.** Clearly, no one knows everything, and yes, your mother or mother-in-law may have raised children before you, but it doesn't mean that you are not entitled to raising your children as you and your partner see fit.

✔ **Keep your boundaries clearly in place and ensure that you remind your friends and family of these.** Be open and transparent. If Grandma puts Fanta in little Jimmy's cup and hopes you won't pipe up in front of 15 guests, do pipe up. But politely, respectfully, and even using humor. It may sound like something like "No, Grandma. Little Jimmy still cannot have Fanta since last week!"

✔ **Keep your distance.** I know it seems counterproductive, but if all else fails, this might be necessary. Not all families and friends are loving and caring, and some are rather toxic. If you happen to be unfortunate and are surrounded by these, and you have tried everything else, keep gatherings to a minimum. You may also find it helpful to only meet at your house or in neutral territory to keep power unbalances at bay, or see these specific friends or relatives with your partner present. You know, strength in numbers and all.

✔ **Limit the amount of help you ask friends or family for who you do not have a good relationship with.** It is hard to say "no" to your sister (or sister-in-law) crashing at your house unannounced when you have just asked her to babysit for a week. Avoid putting yourself in a situation where you may feel like you owe something, as naturally, it will impact on your ability to uphold your decisions and boundaries.

✔ **Don't gossip or spread rumors.** It is human nature to want to vent and seek emotional support, but there are right ways and wrong ways to do it. Talking about your sister-in-law to their mother is unlikely to play out in your favor. Speak to your friends and relatives or to a third party, who has no vested interests in the situation.

✔ **Seek support and make sure you are both handling the situation well.** Go back to the list of problem signs we discussed at the beginning of this chapter, and if you notice any of these, or feel that your partner and yourself may not be coping, make sure you self-care and get support. This may include everything from a hot bath and chocolates, to a massage and seeing a therapist.

What if My Partner Likes His Friends (or Mine) Too Much?

You have met each other's friends, and your partner has genuinely clicked with your best friend or has a best friend that he/she is completely attached to. You start to grow a little paranoid, and you almost feel like a third wheel. Is there a "getting along too much" scenario here? How much is too much? What about the platonic friendship vs. the sexual attraction that you think is there?

There are some clear alarm bells in all relationships, but these go beyond black and white facts. For example, one of my best friends is a male, and we do speak very often, but there never was, and will never be anything else. This is not measured by how often I might see or talk to him, but by how we both feel about our friendship, by how transparent we are about our conversations, and by how comfortable we are talking about our spouses, families, and general conversations.

Firstly, what was your partner and this other person's relationship before you became a couple? Were they close? What did they share or speak about? It would be silly to expect your partner to drop their best friend just because you became a couple. However, having said this, as much as it is about accepting their friendship, it should be clear that the friend has accepted your relationship. It should not be about replacing one another, and the boundaries should be crystal clear. There is a well-defined distinction between the role of a partner and the role of a best friend. One is romantic and sexual, and the other one is 100% platonic. If there any confusion, then there is a need to discuss this friendship and how it fits into your relationship.

Secondly, relationships with other girls/boys are about transparency. Is your partner hiding his relationship with him/her, or is this in the public domain? Is there an element of jealousy/rivalry when you and the best friend run into each other? Make sure to look at it objectively. A lot of the time, how we feel about our partner having a relationship with another male/female says more about how we feel about ourselves and our insecurities than they say about their relationship. Recognize the things that make you feel uncomfortable and make sense of them are in your head. Do you have an issue with your weight, a particular personality trait, or your job? Often, we will react to a trigger and interpret it subjectively based on our thoughts and feelings. This is human, although it may lead to wrong assumptions.

Finally, there are some very practical "guidelines" to having a friendship with someone of the same gender as your partner. These include managing physical contact that is appropriate for you and your partner. For example, in some countries, it is an acceptable social norm to kiss friends on the cheek and absolutely nothing to be concerned about. In other places, physical contact of this type would be considered intimate. It is important to be mindful of what may seem over-familiar in a friendship or potentially taken the wrong way. Things like getting changed in private, discussing appropriate topics, and how a partner speaks of their spouse is important. If a partner found themselves criticizing their other half to their BFF on a regular basis, confusion may develop about the commitment to the romantic relationship, and may slowly send the wrong message to the friend. In short, the level of intimacy between your couple should be much greater than the level of intimacy between a partner and their friend. If this is not the case, I would be asking myself and my partner some questions.

> When I met my (then) boyfriend's girlfriend, I was a bit put off by how they kissed each other hello. That's what they had always done! I didn't have to say anything for them to stop though. They pretty much did on their own after they both got into serious relationships.
>
> Ten years later, we all have kids of the same age and are all very close. My husband and his best friend are still best friends. But no, they don't kiss anymore!

As per every other topic in this book, this discussion is about communication. It is important to be open to discussing relationships of any type with your partner and to raise any concerns. It is also about being kind and understanding. Yes, it might well be that you have kissed your female best friend on the lips platonically since senior year, but it upsets your wife. So be compassionate and stop it.

—> **Chapter 5 Tips** <—

Be True to Yourself. You and your partner come with your unique ways, personalities, insecurities, opinions, and wishes. Those are important, even when they are not perfect. There are things that you will be prepared to negotiate, while there will be some that you won't. Accept these, and accept your needs as real. It is common for individuals to try to change themselves for new friends and in-laws, only to realize six months down the track that they can't sustain that change. It is better to be honest from the first moment than to try to be someone else for a while and fail miserably.

Communicate. As per the motto of this book. Being able to talk about the good, the bad, and the ugly is the most important thing your relationship can do. If you can communicate about your fears, insecurities, values, and thoughts, regardless of what these are, you are in a good place. Being able to negotiate rules and boundaries is also extremely important and draws the line in managing friends and family positively.

Accept Differences. You, your partner, your families, and friends have clear different opinions, values, and personalities. Accept that half the time, you could easily avoid conflict if both parties made an effort to understand the other person's perspective. Compromise and don't sweat the small stuff. In essence, pick your battles, and choose the important over the negligible arguments. Like I said in Chapter 3, you will not win all battles, so you might as well reserve your energy for the important times.

Plan the Good Times. Whether you get along with your families and friends as a couple or not, you need to remember the most important part of this relationship: YOUR relationship. Plan your good times, dates, dreams, and goals, regardless of whether you have loads of friends and relatives on the journey. If you can, plan good times with the extended family and friends too. Relationships take time to build, and it is important to nurture these, especially at the beginning.

In Summary

Relationships with friends and family are usually unavoidable. When you meet your Mr. or Mrs. Right, the odds are that you will meet and be involved with their family. In a perfect world, they will be lovely, you will all gel right away, and everybody will respect everybody's boundaries, rules, and space. However, in the real world, you may need some time to get to know each other. You may struggle with some aspects of the relationships or their personalities. Or they may not accept you right away for who you are. However, generally once the storming phase is out of the way, people start getting along alright. When it comes to relationships between people of the same gender as your partner, it is a tricky to navigate, and it is important to remember basic rules. Communication, respect, and empathy are the key, but first and foremost, even as a small couple in a big world, the most important part of this to nurture is YOU.

CHAPTER 5: TRUTH OR DARE

✔ On a piece of paper, write down three boundaries you think are important. Write each step of the boundary clearly (what it is, how you would let people know, and what natural consequences you would put in place to protect this boundary).

✔ Organize a "date" with a relative or friend of your partner you would like to get to know more (and who you haven't had the chance to bond with).

✔ With your partner, discuss what would be appropriate, and what wouldn't, for your relationship regarding relationships with their BFF. Share your thoughts and boundaries. Then discuss the same for your BFF.

✔ Name one thing that you are struggling with regarding one of the friends/relatives in your relationship (it could be your partner's side or yours). Discuss the reasons and how you could manage it.

✔ Plan a hot date with your lover, just the two of you. Make sure that you both feel loved and special. Remember that your partnership is the most important.

✔ Write a thank-you card to a family member for something they did and show your appreciation.

✔ Watch a movie about crazy in-laws and laugh it off. The truth is, yours probably aren't so bad.

SOCIAL MEDIA IN RELATIONSHIPS

Relationships have evolved. The way we meet people, the manner in which we progress in and out of relationships, and our modern living have influenced our lifestyles. Things like internet hobby groups, online dating platforms, and social media have changed the way we access romantic interests. Once upon a time, if a person wasn't living in your area, attending your local gym, or a friend of a friend, you had almost no chance of meeting them, let alone having a relationship with them. What a contrast to today, where you can meet and socialize with men and women from the comfort of your living room, 100 miles away from them.

For most of us, to feel socially and emotionally fulfilled, we need to develop meaningful relationships outside our immediate relatives. Social media has become that tool to allow people to connect with others without slowing down their lifestyles, having to look too far, and keeping abreast of all the important gossip. Initially, social media groups, like Facebook, were mostly designed for existing relationships to keep in touch. However, we've seen a change in how we use social media. These days, it is as much about creating new connections as it is to keep in touch with existing friends.

> " I can't say that I am an online freak. In fact, I hold way less social media accounts than my peers. And yet, yesterday, I received some random email (where did they get my email from in the first place?) coming from a professional social media group, designed for professionals (supposedly), telling me how beautiful I was and asking to meet!
>
> To the spam folder that went!

According to Pew Research Centre (2017), there is a correlation between social media and relationship dissatisfaction. It is partly linked to feeling pressured to conform with others and constantly comparing our relationship with our friends'. Imagine that you have always wanted to get married, but your partner has never considered it. Watching Jenny, Samantha, Mark, and his cousin Fred's perfect romantic proposals playing on a loop in your newsfeeds is bound to grate at you after a while. It is important to remember that keeping in touch with friends is one thing but to be blinded by romanticized and often exaggerated (if not made up) perfect lives can make yours look dim in comparison. In principle, most of us will know not to believe everything social media throws at us. And yet, most of us will get annoyed, upset, or sad watching what seems to be much better lives than ours. Consequently, we may start being ungrateful, sarcastic, down, or even blame our partner for not giving us the same amount of "perfection" as the hundred screenshots we seem to have stored on our phone. Bluntly, do not look at anything on social media and believe it is real, and do not, I say *do not* allow it to influence how you feel about your relationship.

Another point that was highlighted in the Pew research study, and corroborated by multiple others, is that our permanent access to phones and electronic devices has impacted on the attention we give to our partners while with them. To put it simply, how often do we go out for dinner and whack our phones on the table, reacting to every beep that comes from it? To push this further, how difficult would it be to leave our devices at home, or Heaven forbid, not check them at all for a week? (Is that shock and horror I hear?). Yes, it would be hard. If you're anything like me, your phone and laptop are your mobile office items, and you have a job that requires a lot of you, at all times. Despite this, how can we ensure that we give our partners some undivided attention on a regular basis without being distracted by the habit of social and online networks?

> *My wife and I went out for dinner a couple of weeks ago to a lovely restaurant. We were taken to our table in what seemed a very calm and quiet environment. We sat down and looked around, to see that eight out of the ten couples in our area, in that super expensive and romantic venue, were nose deep in their phones, completely closed off to one another.*
>
> *So, we both laughed and turned our phones off. It was one of the best nights we had in a long time!*

Another common issue for couples in this social-media era revolves around trust, jealousy, and attention-seeking behaviors that may impact on the quality of relationships. Remember what we discussed earlier; watching fake perfect lives can make you feel like you need more in lots of areas. Human nature seeks this. Other times, we may stumble upon it by accident, but do enjoy it when it is there. Considering how easy it is to connect with others on social media, unhappy individuals could easily meet someone else and in them, create a perfect persona to meet all of their unmet fantasies. This creates two issues; for one, people who pine for something perfect based on social-media fantasies may feel an attraction to males or females who are displaying (AKA faking) this perfection. "Onscreen" lovers are easily ideal in comparison to "face-to-face" ones. After all, dirty socks lying around, snoring, farting in their sleep, and eating that last chocolate brownie despite being 10 kilos too heavy can quietly hide behind a pretty cool avatar. Secondly, even if it is that you would never seek another relationship through social media, the existence and access of private messaging, public inter-actions, and 24/7 content may provoke feelings of anxiety, jealousy, and mistrust in partners. It's not unusual for lovers to argue over access to each other's social media. The old "you won't mind if you have nothing to hide" can only go so far. The bottom line is that the use of social media is a double-edged sword, and a lot of couples struggle between trusting their partners vs. being too naïve in noticing things that do not quite make sense.

> *In the early days of our relationship, we might have been more private around online behaviors, but 20 years on, we can't say that we care. In actuality, we both have the same password for all of our accounts (yeah, maybe not bright against hackers) and often play with each other's phones. Privacy is only for pooping and affairs, I reckon!*

The way I look at it is that social media is similar to the other areas of our relationships. Is your partner honest with you? Have they ever done anything to make you question their behavior? Has anything happened lately to make you doubtful? If the answer is a solid no, why would you start being distrusting now? Do you have open and warm communication between you? If yes, why would you not simply discuss your doubts and worries, rather than snooping behind their backs to check on their social media? However, if your partner suddenly only checks his or her social media accounts in the bathroom, has updated their password, or simply has changed towards you, then I would suggest an open conversation about it.

Questionable Online Behaviors in a Relationship

Some behaviors may hurt your relationship. Sometimes, these are accidental and without intent. Other times, we damn well know that they are, but hope to get away with them without too much damage. If you recognize any of them in yourself, consider a good look in front of the mirror to discover why you are doing it. If you notice any of them in your partner, be honest with them and discuss your concerns (or even better, go through this chapter together).

1. Inappropriate Activities

So, you log on to your Instagram account and notice that your partner has liked photos of girls in their underwear, shared pretty explicit illustrations with coworkers, or that your girlfriend has liked the last 20 posts of her ex-boyfriend who, as far as you thought, hated her. Inappropriate activities are pretty broad, and what is inappropriate for one couple may not be for another. However, generally, the couple knows deep down what boundaries they have committed to. I encourage you to have a conversation about these activities with an open mind. After all, all couples deserve the chance to talk things out. But do not bottle it up. Your anxiety, frustration, and resentment will only grow as you watch your partner's activities in a paranoid frame of mind. Rip the Band-Aid off and bring these up. There may well be a completely innocent reason, and it would be a shame to assume the worst for no reason.

2. Privacy Overload

Suddenly, your partner adds facial recognition to his laptop, fingerprinting access on his phone, and changes his passwords to something completely secret. Yep, I will be brave and say that I would be curious, if not concerned, as to what I missed there. I do not necessarily believe that it is healthy to share all passwords and social media accounts access with our partner, but the extreme of *hiding* these are not healthy either and may indicate that your partner requires a high level of privacy. The question is, why? The first step is noticing substantial changes in our partner's behaviors, but the second and vital next step is to communicate with them about it.

3. Privacy Underload

Your partner may be the opposite and not consider anything private. He or she may post everything on social media, like your last meal, toilet break, and latest argument. It is important for couples to be on the same wave length when it comes to how much they want to share and with whom. If your loved one is adding every man and his dogs as "friends" or "connections" on social media, remind them that these people often view all of your content (by default), and therefore, you would appreciate a minimum of privacy. Also, let your partner know if you notice posts or photos that make you feel uncomfortable, especially if they are of you.

4. Attention Seeking Much

How much attention are you and your partner comfortable with? I mentioned earlier about my pet hate of people posting "perfect" lives on social media, when we know that they are far from perfect, sometimes even far from being happy. If your partner is constantly posting photos of your perfect relationship, or thanking you for the moon when you are regularly arguing, point out to them the discrepancy between their fake social media life vs. the real one they're ignoring. The opposite also applies. If your partner is posting about your latest romantic massage and how grateful they genuinely were, but you didn't want the world to know, let him or her know.

> *My boyfriend kept posting photos of himself, shirtless in all poses and situations. It drove me completely crazy. I warned him that if he kept going, I would do the same. He kept*

going. So, I posted a photo of me in sexy underwear, suspenders and all, sitting on his motorbike while he was at work. He rushed home in less than 17 minutes and made me take it down. He was completely and utterly possessively mad!

He sure learned his lesson but never found out that I had manipulated my Facebook settings so that no one but him could see that photo!

Attention seeking can take other forms too. Sometimes it's not about your relationship, but about individual bragging rights. For example, if you find out that your partner is posting to get extra attention, and it is making you feel embarrassed, let him or her know. Yes, we know that little Jimmy is smart, but how many times do we need to hear about their wonderful achievements, over and over again? We accept that someone might be smart, pretty, or successful, but solely reading about their amazing grades, new book, or pseudo health concerns can be draining on the relationship. Point these out to your partner and make sure that you communicate your thoughts and concerns objectively and respectfully.

5. Social Media Marathon

We discussed the addictive nature of social media earlier. Therefore, it is important to note the importance of offline moments with your partner too. Make a point to leave your phones behind (or go offline) when you are on a date, when discussing important topics, or when being intimate. Maybe pick a time where you are both allowed to binge on your social media accounts and share content with each other, and pick a time where you are forbidden to do so. The rest is somewhat in the middle and you should negotiate it in your relationship.

So yes, there are some behaviors with social media that can put pressure and tension in your relationship, but I do not think it would be fair to blame social media alone. It is important to remember our role in managing our online habits, and as per every other chapter of this book, show positive and good communication skills with your partner. Of course, it is also important to remember that we can use social media to improve or maintain awesome relationships too.

→ Chapter 6 Tips ←

Catfishing. If you have never watched the MTV show Catfish, you have to. It is the funniest online dating show I have ever watched. In short, the show hosts, Nev and Max, provide support to individuals who have fallen in love with online entities. They travel around the States to help the lovers to meet. The sad reality is that it almost always turns out that the other person behind the screen is a fake to the dismay of their online partner. Therefore, for this chapter, I encourage you to be weary of catfishes. If you are in an online relationship with someone whom you have never met, be careful. There is almost always a reason they do not want to meet you. As we discussed earlier, it is easy to make ourselves and appear perfect from behind a screen. Be smart, and if you have met someone online, make sure to go and meet them face-to-face to continue your romance.

Beware of Addictions. The issue with social media, and with the various online platforms we all have access to these days, is that they can lead to addictions. These may include addictions to social media itself, addictions to attention-seeking behaviors, addictions to games (I am told that Candy Crush is pretty good), and gambling addictions.

Like with any addictions, we only notice them when we cannot access them. Things seem fine until our internet is down, we have dropped our phone in the bathtub, or that we have run out of money for the latest bet. Be observant if you notice that your partner exhibits these traits. Ask for help if you are exhibiting these traits. These can be detrimental to your mental health and your relationship. Being free from addictions is important for a happy life.

Use Social Media Well. Social media can be wonderful in sharing information, photos, and updates with friends and family, particularly those who do not live nearby. Make good use of social media with the people in your lives. Share your latest vacation with Aunty Gertrude who lives in the UK, say, "G'day, mate" to your second cousin from Australia, share an article on the good vine with your vineyard-lover dad, or invite your sister to your next girls' night. Make good use of social media.

Improve Our Romance through Social Media. Who said that couples cannot use social media to add romance to their relationship? Things like sharing love hearts, sending messages to your partner during your lunch break, sending video clips of their favorite TV series, or playing games can be both fun and loving. Does your partner love puppies? Then share that cute photo of a husky in the snow. Does your partner enjoy cooking meals from scratch? Then show them that video about growing herbs and veggies. Make use of the various online features that could contribute to an exciting love life.

In Summary

Social media is a modern invention that has revolutionized the way humans connect, communicate, and live in today's world. Unfortunately, it has come with a variety of tricky elements amongst the great ones we all seem to enjoy. It is important to navigate these, as individuals and as couples, to ensure that we use them to improve our lives and our relationships rather than to complicate and damage the connections we have with the real people in our lives.

Having said that, it is important to say that many people have connected and fallen in love via social media. Whether through online dating, common online friends, or as part of similar online groups, we live in a society where a lot of our living occurs through the internet. It is important to recognize the value of social media in keeping in touch with friends and relatives, in meeting potential love interests, and to give me my daily serve of attention. Remember that you can also connect with me on social media.

CHAPTER 6: TRUTH OR DARE

✔ Swap phones with your partner and spend 10 minutes on their various social media, getting interested in what they are liking, posting, and sharing.

✔ Pick a photo on social media and discuss with your partner whether the photo is appropriate for you. Discuss why and why not. Remember that it is not about the right answer, but about sharing thoughts.

✔ Choose a social media platform and open your friends' list. Allow your partner to ask about a random number of connections. Describe how you know them, the level of contact you have with them, and anything you both might find relevant. Then swap turns. Remember that this exercise is not about checking on your partner, but opening a dialogue on your social media habits.

✔ If you are in an online relationship, make a day and time to meet. Make sure to balance the online with the real.

✔ If you are having some concerns about your partner's online behaviors, let them know. Ask yourself whether there are troubling signs or whether you could be over-reacting.

✔ Disconnect yourself from all online account for 24 hours. If you are having withdrawals, consider your level of online addiction.

✔ Next time you are going on a date with your partner, leave your phones at home or in the car (or turn them off and leave them in your bag/pocket).

PART THREE

Why Did We Want This Again?

PREGNANCY

Congratulations on the Good News!

Well, that is the polite thing to say, right? The truth is that you are about to embark on a crazy ride that will make you question your sanity. So, congratulations on the most stressful, time-consuming, work-giving, fight-causing, and life-changing news of your life. But none of us would change it regardless. Having a baby will change your life, but with good preparation and a good sense of humor, you will do amazingly.

Before we start, I completely recognize that some people embark on single parenting purposely. I also wish to acknowledge individuals in relationships who may be having a baby through a surrogate or same-sex couples who may not be physically pregnant while awaiting a baby. However, for this chapter, we will be mentioning topics concerning pregnancy where one of the partners is physically pregnant, though, of course, I hope that the content in this chapter may be useful to all parents-to-be, regardless of their situation.

For most couples, deciding to have a baby comes following some form of emotional commitment, though for some others, the baby surprised them and led to a promise of a happy ending. Either way, I don't know that couples fully comprehend the level of change their relationship will undertake. Not only will you have to share your time, love, and attention with a new person (and a very needy new person), you will also have to do it under duress, sleep deprivation, drowned in chores, and with half the money you used to have. Okay, I accept that I may not be painting the most positive light of pregnancy and parenting, and you may even ask "why on earth would anyone do it?" I have asked myself the same question in the last few years, after birthing a soccer team who all drive me crazy at the best of times. I guess the truth is that when night time comes, and I have played tickle with my 9-year-old, sang our goodnight song with my 11-year-old, or received a good night hug from my 13-year-old, I feel warm and fuzzy and I go to bed knowing why I did it.

I am often asked by people whether they are ready, the timing is right, their relationship is strong enough, or they should have a baby. I do not know the answer to any of this. The reason being that no one is fully ready, a good timing does not guarantee that things will not go wrong, and having a baby is such a huge commitment that no one should breed because they feel pressured to do so. However, some things may be useful to know before you decide to get pregnant, and during your pregnancy, to prepare you for the ride. Here a few topics to get you and your partner thinking.

I Say Yes. He Says No.

You have been in a relationship for a while, and you have seriously considered bringing a baby into your relationship. You have already pictured the pink (or blue) little outfits, shortlisted a bunch of names, and even visited your local nursery school. You have organized a great dinner, and finally, you spit it out and ask your partner how they would feel about having a little bundle of joy before you are greeted by a "no way," followed by "wanna pass the TV remote?"

We can imagine that the night would take on a different turn to what you had expected, unfortunately.

Most couples progressively discuss offspring through their relationship. It might happen to you after watching cousin Sarah parade her baby son for 6 hours or while strolling past the formula aisle of your local supermarket. Start dropping hints if you think that you might want to take the next step in your relationship. Bring the topic up casually in conversation, and start letting your partner know that you are thinking about it. Topics such as the number children, age gaps, maternity leave versus returning to work, and lifestyles choices will generally follow. For most of us, huge topics, such as pregnancy and parenting, need to sink in. For others, they have known most of their lives that they wanted a boy followed by a girl two years later while living in a country house guarded by a German Sheppard. To start with, have a casual, non-threatening conversation before having a very serious sit-down meeting about pregnancy wishes. After that, it is about positive, respectful, and open conversations, and I invite you to practice the tools we discussed in Chapters 2 and 3 and apply them to pregnancy decisions.

Ready, Set, Go!

Firstly, at the risk of contradicting myself, I would like to explain that being ready for a baby can make a positive difference. Things like having space, stability, and finances are significant. For example, though I had my first two children in a moldy 30-meter square apartment a few months before moving to the other side of the world, I would say that decorating a nursery, for instance, is a pretty cool milestone of pregnancy. It is not to say that a baby would notice where it slept or even care, but you might. Having your baby come home to a less than ideal environment, where the purchase of diapers and formula is tricky, or in a relationship that is on the verge of splitting up, may not be the best idea. As I said, it doesn't mean it is doomed, as my first two children will testify, but it is making a hard journey even harder. If you are planning your baby, enjoy the preparations. If your baby is a surprise, I believe you can still plan as much as you can for your upcoming bundle of joy to alleviate some of the ups and downs coming your way.

Getting Pregnant—The Fun Part?

Getting pregnant is supposed to be fun. And it is, for the couples who get pregnant easily. For the others, getting pregnant can include daily temperature checks, ovulation kits, very robotic lovemaking, and a high level of monthly despair. Be aware that the mechanics of *trying* to get pregnant can be draining. Nothing like a call during a business meeting, asking you to come home "cause now is the time" is sure to incite sexy romance.

It is not always better for females. You might be excited the first time your temperature peaks, but after 30 times a month, taking your temperature only to watch it rollercoaster in some unpredictable pattern is bound to kill your after-sex glow. So yes, trying to get pregnant is exciting, but could take longer than predicted and could turn lovemaking into a bit of a chore. If you are one of those couples who are actively trying to get pregnant, consider how you could keep up the romance (see Chapter 13 on intimacy and keeping your sex life alive). Be considerate of your partner's emotions. It is common for couples, particularly women, to feel a sense of biological self-esteem loss when unable to get pregnant. Remember to self-care and to show love and attention.

> *If anyone had told me the nightmare getting pregnant would have been, I would have bailed! We spent more on ovulation kits and fertility apps than we did on anything else in that time. And that's not talking about the monthly wailing of my wife in front of the biggest ice cream tub I could find. Seriously, it was hell. And one day, it happened. And then it happened three times after that, and now we sort of laugh it off, wishing getting pregnant would be harder!*

Men and Women's Businesses

When it comes to the crunch, it is important to have support. Sometimes that support comes from our partner. Sometimes it cannot. In particular, sometimes our irrational anxiety or fears only hurt or freak out our loved one. After all, that would be counterproductive, particularly if they are prone to freaking out about irrational thoughts once you have put them in their head. For example, let's say that you were worried about your vagina ripping from head to toe through the delivery, or as a partner, questioned whether you even wanted to be in the delivery room. These questions are reasonable questions but may stir emotions in yourself and your partner without enough time or the opportunity to process them. You might find that your mother, sister, cousin, or best friend, who all had children, might be able to reassure you on "women's business."

As a male, you might find that talking to a friend around a cold beer is a better approach for you. As I said, by no means am I implying that you should not communicate to your partner. What I am saying is that there are topics where talking to someone else is best, especially if the topic is stress-inducing for the other half.

We Did It!

Congratulations! You made it to the pregnancy. You or your partner peed on a stick and discovered you were going to be a mom or a dad. You and your partner probably felt a lot of mixed emotions: excitement, fear, anxiety, love, and confusion. The way men and women process their emotions, and particularly around pregnancy, is quite different. Depending on whether one of the partners wanted the pregnancy more than the other, you might find that one of you seems to be more focused on specific areas (i.e., finances versus breastfeeding). This is okay. Sometimes until you see the baby on an ultrasound, and sometimes even until it is born, neither parents fully relate to it. Other times, it is the opposite and partners can be over the moon from beginning to the end. A lot is bound to happen and change in the next nine months.

Almost There

Most couples somewhat discuss birthing before the big day. The extent to which they talk about it can differ between relationships, and certainly depends on whether this is a first pregnancy or not, but the key here to prepare. In my experience, men and women who attend a birth, without knowing what they're in for, generally struggle in their relationship after the birth. This is partly as a result of shock, trauma, emotional disconnection, or good old resentment. Regardless, it is vital to consider the birds and the bees talk all the way to taking the baby home *before* the big day. Take my word for it; birthing can be as harrowing as it can be incredible. Though there are elements we cannot control, and these are real, there are many we can. Partners, make sure to listen to your woman, reassure her, give her what she needs, and be prepared to go all caveman (or cavewoman) on those who get in her way until your baby is born and life starts returning to something a bit more normal. (I said "something" a bit more normal; I did not say "normal." FYI, normal has left your vocabulary when you became pregnant and embarked on parenthood.)

> *As soon as the birth started, everything we had discussed or learned went out the window. I tried to be the model birthing partner, though apparently even holding her hand wasn't done the right way!*
>
> *But stripping down to my underwear and jumping in the shower with her scored me the title of "boyfriend of the year." She still tells her friend about it! It was a pretty special moment.*

→ Chapter 7 Tips ←

Metamorphosis. When you wake up this morning, take a good look at yourself and your partner in the mirror. The odds are that the people you see in the mirror will be gone soon, to be replaced by *parents*. Parenting is incredible in changing people. It makes us consider the universe, the fragility of our existence, and our purpose, and helps us see beyond ourselves. Things that previously were important to your lifestyle, things such as sleep-ins, extended holidays, specific purchases, and your general outlook on life, will completely be replaced by baby-related needs. In a very blunt sense, the things you spoiled yourself with previously will appear *selfish*. Your relationship with your partner will change too.

Pre-pregnancy, the world revolved around the two of you. What you wanted to do, where you wanted to go, and your dreams and goals. Suddenly, you put your needs on the backburner, and for some partners, they describe almost feeling replaced by the baby to come. Therefore, it is important at this stage of your life to consider your family balance. Let go of your lifestyle ideals and prepare for the most important person in your future.

Remember that children do grow up, and you do not want to wake up in 20 years having lost all interest and common points with your partner. Have faith that there is a time and a season for everything, and yes, the next few years will be about the baby. However, you will remain a partnership, even in raising this child, so how can you metamorphose into the best of both worlds?

> *I got pregnant through IVF as planned with my girlfriend (she carried our first baby), and I truly love them both. God knows I do. But I didn't expect that level of bonding with my pregnant belly. That gut wrenching, animalistic, need to put this baby first was overwhelming!*
>
> *My girlfriend felt a bit left out, and for a while, we had to really make an effort. But it worked out fine. Six years on, we have a beautiful daughter and a beautiful son, and a relationship stronger than ever. But yes, we had to fight over who would change the dirty diapers like everybody else before we got there!*

Hormones. Pregnancy hormones are well known to influence thoughts and feelings. As you (or your partner) grow into this pregnancy, you might find yourself (or your pregnant lover) to be more and more irritable, anxious, restless, or even needy. Before you roll your eyes, let me ask you how you would feel if we injected you with a cocktail of hormones, enough for at least two people, on a daily basis? How would you feel if an alien had taken over your belly, keeping you up, peeing constantly, and short of breath at the best of times? Finally, how would you feel if you felt like an elephant, and a tipsy one at that, while your partner continued with his or her energetic lifestyle in a body perfectly in control? Alright, I have made my point, so I trust you to be understanding to your baby-making partner.

> *OMG. I had no idea that my wife would turn into the girl in The Exorcist. I kid you not. It was THAT bad. Just visualize my wife, my happy wife, possessed by a demon able to turn her into a demanding, tear-stricken, needy monster. And yet, as she would sleep, a mask of contentment on her face, her belly wobbling from my son dancing inside her. I knew I wanted this. I wanted this woman and this child like I never wanted anything else in my life.*

Wavelength. Once you have processed the news that a baby is on its way, you may develop particular ideas on what you want for your newborn, how you may decorate the nursery, the brand of diapers you might buy, or cast a particular vote on organic home-made baby purees. Nothing like pregnancy to throw you into an overthinking mode. After all, it is important to decide on which school little Sarah will attend now, isn't it? Alright, maybe not. It is common for couples to go through a mix of emotions during pregnancy, as the mom becomes overprotective of her pregnant belly, and go from feeling extremely close to extremely annoyed at each other.

I have many therapy clients who shared with me that before that first pregnancy, and despite years of relationship, they had never argued. It seems that it changed drastically after that. However, this is all normal and part of the relationship rollercoaster through the lifespan. The key is to understand that men and women attach differently, and in particular, the pregnant partner tends to feel much more maternal in the early stages than her non-pregnant partner. Therefore, if you are pregnant, make sure to include your partner and understand that it might feel different for someone who doesn't feel the baby as it might for you. If you are not pregnant, show excitement and patience for your miracle, even if it doesn't always feel real at the moment.

> " *My girlfriend would wake me up to four times a night and yell "look! Look" and point at something on her belly. Now the first couple of times, I'd look but really wouldn't see anything. After a while, I would just mumble and pat her back to sleep. How many times can we look at nothing, right?*
>
> *Until one day, her belly punched me in the back! And she didn't even wake up!*

Intimacy. Your sex life will most definitely change when you become pregnant. For some, intimacy will be the last thing on your mind. Between morning sickness, aches and pains, feeling fat and bloated, lack of sleep, and general fatigue, the planets may struggle to align for the both of you. It is important for couples not to take their lack of sex as personal, and to make the time to be intimate in other ways. For example, cuddles, belly rubs, feet massage, or simply lying down together while sharing stories about your day can be powerful too. For other couples, sex will be great during the pregnancy, even greater than before. So if this is you, I suggest you limit your bragging to your less lucky-friends.

In Summary

Pregnancy is one of the biggest life-changing events that a couple can go through. It is very similar to Pandora's Box; bringing so much joy and pride to couples, and yet bringing so much anxiety, stress, and fear. This is frightening, and yet, normal. I have yet to meet a pregnant or parenting couple who did not experience a *transition*. If you are considering having a baby, picture your life in five years with real changes to look forward to. If you have not bolted yet, you are doing well. But on a more serious note, pregnancy is a miracle. No matter how your baby comes into your life, I welcome you into the most powerful journey in the world.

CHAPTER 7: TRUTH OR DARE

✔ Have sex for fun. Enjoy it, do not talk about your temperature chart, or think of your perfect position, and relax during the moment. Hard, but not impossible.

✔ Picture yourself, and your relationship, with children in five or ten years' time. What do you see? How is your life similar or different? How do you feel? Are you excited or are you completely turned off? There is no right and wrong; this is simply an exercise to help you process your decision-making.

✔ Write the following words on a piece of paper and fold them in little balls. Then pick one with your partner and discuss your thoughts on the topic together. Use the skills learned in Chapters 2 and 3 to help (words are career, house chores, finances/budget, sex, night feeds, baby names, and values).

✔ Give yourself permission to meet with the boys or the girls and ask any questions you would like to know about pregnancy or birthing, without feeling anxious or embarrassed asking in front of your partner. Get support for anything that may be on your mind that you have not felt comfortable talking about in your relationship.

✔ Give your pregnant partner a massage, or something nice to make her feel good about her transforming body.

✔ Stock up the fridge with craving foods (a happy pregnant girl can only be good, right?).

✔ Organize a date for your partner while you can (both partners should do this). Enjoy the freedom, the stress-free evening, and the compulsory sleep in the next day.

Chapter 8

PARENTING

Welcome to the parenting chapter of *The REAL Guide to Life as a Couple*. This is another important topic for couples to read and consider. While pregnancy is a huge step, and definitely something life-changing in relationships, it only lasts nine months as opposed to parenting (which lasts more like nine decades). Therefore, it is relevant to spend a bit of time considering the ups and the downs of bringing up little people. As I explained in the pregnancy chapter, not all couples will want to have babies. Bringing up children is one of the hardest tasks men and women can engage in, and requires energy, patience, resources, motivation, and sacrifice. It is not a job for those who are not sure that this is something that they truly desire. There is also pressure in society for couples to breed as a logical next step in a good and healthy relationship. Comments like "when are you having a baby?" or "you've been together long enough" *are typical around the Christmas dinner table, particularly coming from* long-lost relatives you have not seen since you were 17. So, before we continue, remember that you are entitled to your life decisions, and no one should make you want to become a parent. However, if this is something that you have decided to do, congratulations on the big, exciting step. In this chapter, we will explore some of the journey you may go through as partners as you embark on the parenting journey.

In movies, it is not unusual for heroes and heroines (of both the same and opposite genders) to go off into the sunset, their new baby in tow, and for them all to live happily ever after. In movies, though, babies do not cost anything, sleep through the night, do not projectile vomit sour milk, and certainly do not kill your sex drive. No, in real life, children are messy, have tantrums, cause parents to lose it on a regular basis, and yes, transform date nights into baked-beans-on-toast nights. I have yet to meet a couple who did not have their stress levels quadrupled after having children, except a wealthy couple who had a cook, a cleaner, and a nanny. From a human behavior point of view, when people are stressed, they lose patience and snap, and their cognitive processing (the way they think) is altered. To add to this, parents are often sleep deprived, exhausted from cleaning, washing, preparing meals, and driving the family around. This level of fatigue can lead to resentment, frustration, and even despair. No wonder the birth of a child is known as the biggest challenge couples can face. In fact, according to the Relationship Research Institute (2017), 70% of couples describe a rapid decline in their relationship satisfaction after the birth of their first child. Scary, isn't it?

> When I was pregnant, I pictured us at the park, pushing our angelic boy in his stroller, watching the beautiful Autumn leaves fall all around us as we held our hands in blessed harmony.
>
> What we got was a crying baby who needed a diaper change every five minutes, a partner who walked five metres ahead of us to damper the noise levels, and the leaves were drenched from a month of torrential rain!

Parenting is not just about babies and toddlers. Parenting is also about raising growing children: driving the family taxi, bodyguarding at parties, breathalyzing before handing car keys over, and nagging teenagers until they get a proper job. On a positive note though, the exhaustion and the level of work involved with younger children will almost disappear as they grow up (keyword here: *almost*), and your life as a couple, and as parents, will transform again. Things like being awake at 5 am for the first feed of the day may be replaced by midlife crisis nightclubbing, followed by a hip replacement. Alright, hopefully not for another 20 years. However, what will happen is that your precious little one will become his or her own person. They will start having an opinion and make choices for themselves, and through it all, you will beg the universe to give you the strength to guide them without chaining them to a bed until their 40th birthday.

So, we have indeed established that parenting is stressful and that the consequences of having children, such as the loss of income, topical differences of opinions, and the increase in chores and responsibilities does impact on how you may communicate or relate to your partner. There is a way out of this parenting maze. Otherwise, 100% of couples would be divorced or separated after a couple of kids. Some of the common survival tips, as described by parents, fall into the categories below.

1. Time for You as a Couple

What generally happens after a while is that parents get into pretty good routines with the family that do not leave a lot of time for "extras." Therefore, the first thing that goes out the window is "us time." Things like adult dinner parties, heart-to-heart conversations, romantic gestures, dressing up for special occasions, Friday night tennis, and sex become rare occurrences. Further, *couples* suddenly become *parents*, and everything starts to revolve around little Jimmy. If you do not keep up with your romantic partner, there may come a time where you will not remember how to be adults together, let alone lovers. There is a real danger in *only* being little Jimmy's mom or dad. Before long, you could find yourself not owning mascara, a tie, or remember what turns your partner on. Make sure that you free up some alone time (and we are not only talking about intimacy here, but time to make jokes, watch a DVD in bed together, or take up a fun activity), and do not forget that you are more than *just* little Jimmy's parent.

> *You know something is going really wrong in life when your wife starts calling you "daddy." Like seriously? Seriously? How creepy is that?*
>
> *Well, not as creepy as the time I replied to her with "yes, mummy."*

2. Fatigue

As I mentioned above, one of the worse culture shocks about going from a single couple to a family revolves around the lack of sleep, in conjunction with the increased workload. Both partners may struggle to adjust to walking like zombies, and in a desperate bid to sleep may, therefore, become angry at their spouse for not taking on whatever chore. Humans tend to lash out when they feel hopeless. It is important to try to communicate positively, and not to personalize any comments that may come out of half-asleep bodies who are feeling tortured and begging for a rest. Things that might be helpful for couples could be to take turns on the night shift, spread the chores evenly (we will discuss chores in Chapter 9), get a babysitter when you can, or forget the cleaning and the non-essential chores. Bluntly, sleep when you can.

3. Sex

Although we will discuss intimacy in part four of this book, one of the biggest complaint from couples, both males and females, revolves around the redefinition of sex during pregnancy, breastfeeding, and parenting. Let me tell you that no matter how attractive you and your partner might be, no matter how turned on you might have been in the past, there is something unique about sex between two sleep-deprived robots, soggy cuddles from leaking breasts, and the romantic ambiance of crying in the background. Yep, post-pregnancy sex is something that couples need to adjust to. A little adaptation such as catching the perfect moment when the moment is perfect goes a long way. Yes, intimacy can be challenging for new parents. Goodbye, exotic places (I suspect the kitchen table will be out of bounds for a while), hello, flexible timing (what is the baby's sleep schedule again?), and welcome to overlooking the details (you don't mind this breastfeeding bra, do you?). However, sex between two loving people will always be beautiful, so don't get hung up on the temporary variances. Make the time to remain intimate as intimacy will relax you and make you feel connected in the midst of madness.

> " *So, there we were, in the throes of passion, after almost five weeks of no sex. Trust me, we were both quite into it. When suddenly, my husband freezes and stares at my chest. Now I knew my "girls" were pretty swollen but that stare...*
>
> *A mix of horror and of contained laughs.*
>
> *My boobs were squirting milk like there was no tomorrow. Squirting like water guns. Not my hottest moment!*

4. Parenting Wavelength

So, picture this. You're taking little Johnny to the mall to shop for his birthday. As you enter the toy shop, surely you have an idea of what you're looking for. Is it a bear? Is it a truck? Is it an abacus? Little Johnny is very bright. He will like any of those. However, *shock horror!* As you turn around, your partner has picked the biggest toy gun he could find, and little Johnny has already faked killed three senior citizens to the great pride of Mr. Dad.

Didn't think of that scenario as you were watching *The Brady Bunch,* did you? Well, it is a good thing that we are talking about parenting wavelength then.

Whether it is about the baby's name, the input of grandparents, what bedding to buy, or where this bedding should sit, you and your partner won't agree on everything. Parents often feel passionate about their ideas and values when it comes to their offspring. When the children grow up, values-based opinions will surface. For example, religious beliefs, discipline, boundaries, education, the input of relatives, choices of friends, choices of schools, pocket money, chores, and even the type of clothes your children will wear will have the potential to match, or mismatch, your partner's radar. Be prepared to be open-minded and willing to discuss your opinions.

I hope that by now, you see the importance of the first section of this book. Two parents who seem to hold contradictory values, and who do not know how to communicate or negotiate, are bound to struggle. Think of the skills you have learned in Section 1 of this guide. How could you use them to assist you both in meeting halfway and seeing each other's point of view? Remember that in most cases, there is no right or wrong. However, in some cases, parenting needs to be taught. If this is the case for your family, that is okay. Arrange a parenting course or see a professional. Parenting, both as a couple and individually, does not come with a manual.

5. Guilt, Worry, and Obsession

It is not unusual for parents to describe parenting as an ongoing guilt trip. A train ride that only stops at Worryland, Worryville, and Saint Worry stations. A trip where there are no road maps and no one able to give you guaranteed pointers for this new journey of yours. Parenting is one of those things. In fact, I can't think of anything else in life which causes as much anxiety and uncertainty over decades. Wondering what the *right* answer is, whether you are causing some long-term damage to your precious child, or freaking out at every newsflash that shows sad and scary incidents.

You can alleviate some of that guilt and worry by accepting that parents can only try their best. Accept that you may—let me rephrase this—you WILL mess up. You WILL make mistakes, and your kid will blame you for something at some point in their life.

Accept this, grieve this, and move on. The fact that you care and want to try your best means your little one is already in great hands. However, if you find yourself so anxious that it stops you from functioning and enjoying the simple things, please seek help. You should expect a degree of rational and even irrational freak-outs. Anything constant, long-term, and that impacts on your quality of time needs to be looked at.

⟶ Chapter 8 Tips ⟵

Prepare Well. As we discussed in the previous chapter, the better prepared you are for parenthood, the less shocked you might feel. Though there is a part of you that will never prepare fully, to read about how other couples have navigated their relationship through this stage of life can be helpful. The same applies to information about birthing, feeding your baby, bonding with your child, and other transformation coming your way. There are lots of helpful books about parenting. However, you might prefer talking to other parents who have been there before you. Simply find ways to learn about what's ahead, in a way that works for you.

Be Supportive. As I have very clearly pointed out in this chapter, becoming a parent is an extremely challenging mission that goes on for decades. While you may have been extremely close pre-baby, you may find that the post-baby relationship is tenser (or not). If this is the case, remember that this is normal, and not something to take personally. Be supportive of your partner. Consider their adjustment, their stress, and their lack of energy following the arrival of your bundle of joy. Now, by no means does this mean that you should do it all on your own, or put up with aggressive behavior. No, it simply means that by being patient, supportive, and accepting that you are both on this journey together, you will do better than if you are walking it on your own.

Seek Help. We all have heard the saying, "It takes a village to raise a child." It is true. Help comes in different formats. For some, it might be financial. A grandparent may slip you an envelope as a "welcome to the world" for your baby. For others, you may get delivered a warm cooked meal that smells like Heaven, from your childhood best friend. You may get free babysitting by your older brother, or you may see a child health nurse weekly to chat about breastfeeding. You may see a therapist or a life coach to work on your family adjustment as a preventative measure, or you may join an online support group for new moms or dads. In any event, help is there and available. Do not ever think that seeking support is a sign of weakness. In my books, it is a sign of smartness.

1+1 = Love. The relationship comes first. Focus on your partnership, not just the parents you have become. Though there are a time and season for everything, and though the next decade (or two) might indeed be about the children, do not completely forget to nurture your relationship. Make a regular date, take time for little romantic gestures, help each other out with the children and various chores. Look forward to your whole life together and continue to grow as lovers.

Forgive Yourself for the Past, Present, and Future. As long as we are alive, we will remain imperfect. We make mistakes, we learn from them, we improve, and then we do it all again. There is no perfect parenting, and unfortunately, though, there are recognized parenting techniques that are deemed best, the odds are that you will not master them at all times. Do not be so critical of yourself that it cripples you. Conversely, forgive yourself, recognize opportunities to do better next time, and do like all other parents before you; practice it all on your first kid.

Enjoy It. Despite all the frightening information in this chapter (good enough to attract a family planning sponsor), being a parent has some cool aspects. There is something instinctual about looking at your child in the eyes for the first time, knowing that there will forever be an unbreakable bond. There is something priceless about watching your flesh and blood develop into people with their personalities, and cracking up at their own priceless (if not predictable) jokes. Family dinners will take on a completely different feel. Over time, the sound of wailing will be replaced by the sound of laughter, love, and commitment to each other. Being part of a family is a privilege and, though the first few years are extremely difficult, there is light at the end of the tunnel, particularly when your kids save you from the nursing home option.

> *As a mother of two children, I tried my best twice. With my first, I was strict. Now I find myself with an overly emotive teenager. With the second, I was much more lenient. However, I am finding myself with an attention-seeker who thinks the world spins around her!*
>
> *I should have had a third one to see if I could get it right in the middle!*

In Summary

Pregnancy and parenting are often described as one of the main sources of relationship stress. In my experience working with couples, this is often the case. Communicating around those issues is the key. This chapter only briefly touched on some of the common issues couples face in parenting, and that is because the key isn't in the issues but in our ability to reflect on them, as well as our willingness to talk about them. So, hug it out. Watch out for the chapters on chores and responsibilities that will cover finances in raising children, as well as explore how couples may share the workload while the chapter on intimacy will delve deeper on the ways couples can keep their relationship exciting.

Consider that while parenting is one of the best things on earth, it is also one of the hardest. Be aware of the support available, reach out if you need to, and be there for your spouse. Be patient, be kind to yourself, and enjoy the ride.

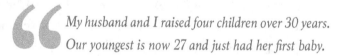

My husband and I raised four children over 30 years. Our youngest is now 27 and just had her first baby.

I can honestly say we are reaping the fruits of our hard labor now. Imagine being able to have your cake and eat it too? Well this is what being a grandparent feels like. Feed the kids junk food, hype them up, spoil them, then give them back!

Definitely makes parenting all worth it!

CHAPTER 8: TRUTH OR DARE

✔ With your partner, pick an age for a child and write three presents you would think of getting him or her. Then share your ideas and discuss.

✔ Write down three traditions from your childhood you loved and would like to continue with your own family. Explain them to your partner.

✔ Offer to take over a child/house chore for your partner with a good heart (and do it).

✔ When feeling worried, stressed, or anxious, practice a relaxation exercise. A simple one might be to ground your feet and relax all of your muscles. Then, take ten deep breaths.

✔ Prepare a fun, romantic, restful, or exciting date with your partner. Do not tell them what it is and surprise them with a child-free night.

✔ Write yourself a letter. In the letter, write about your struggle as a parent, your happy moment, and forgive yourself for everything in between. Genuinely find peace in doing your best.

✔ However, if there are things that you should seek help for as a parent (which go beyond the regular issues), then do it. I know that it is scary to acknowledge these, but I promise you that it is worth it.

✔ While your children are asleep (or get a babysitter), go to bed with your partner. Have sex, relax in front of a movie, or take a nap. Enjoy the simple things.

✔ Make older children do chores for you. If they can walk, they'll make the cut.

CHORES AND RESPONSIBILITIES

I don't know if you enjoyed the TV show *Little House on the Prairie* as much as I did, but I would like to bring the story up in this very relevant chapter. In short, the show highlighted very simple, fulfilling, and happy lives, in warm and caring communities. However, it was all very stereotypical for the times. Husbands did all the physical chores, wives did all the cooking, cleaning, and the raising of children, while the offspring, of course, were all perfectly quiet, polite, and well-kempt (except Nancy, of course, for the fans of the show). Same-sex relationships did not exist in the series or at least they didn't mention them. There were never any arguments or questions about role expectations. People just did what their gender assigned them to do, and as such, they lived their lives until they all died.

Now, we can see how we have evolved, and how *Little House on the Prairie* in today's time would cause a few riots. How could women be responsible for all the house chores, as well as all the parenting, when in 95% of the time, they are also working, studying, or involved in various projects? How is it that men should not enjoy cooking every night, or be looked down upon for being at-home fathers? Though we have become better at challenging stereotypes, there are still many modern households that believe that there are "men" and "women" jobs. Can you guess from this list which chores would stereotypically be assigned to which gender?

✔ Car servicing, lawn mowing, cooking, grocery shopping, cleaning, budgeting, bill payments, and (Heaven forbid) ironing.

If you look at your parents' relationship, do you notice patterns of gender stereotypes, or is it more modern and equal? What about your relationship? Would you say that it is very typical, and if so, why?

> *I remember the early days. My boyfriend and I had just moved in together. I thought I'd be nice and fold some washing, but when he came home, he complained that it wasn't done properly and redid it all!*
>
> *That's the last time I did washing! And guess who became the washing king to his great surprise? My boyfriend!*

If we look beyond the stereotypes, we see other factors that drive who will be doing chores, or be responsible for particular aspects of the relationship. Remember Chapter 1 on temperament and personalities? Perfect time to bring it up. Some partners are more persistent around what they like or do not like to do. Others are more flexible or easy going. For example, if you hate doing the dishes, but do not feel that strongly about it, the odds are that you will probably not fight too hard against it, and you'll be doing the dishes for the next couple of decades. However, if you hate doing the dishes, believe that it's a woman (or man)'s job, and have a tendency to be on the stubborn side, the odds are that doing the dishes will be a source of arguments. Now, there are enough chores in one household to keep both partners occupied, and as long as they both agree on it, there is nothing wrong in having set chores for each. In many relationships, one partner may be responsible for cooking all the meals for example, while the other ensures that all bills get paid. In other relationships, it's more about taking turns with the various assignments. As I said, it is not so much about the chores, but about the division of labor and whether both partners believe the arrangement is fair and viable. Simply put, how do we split chores and responsibilities in our changing times?

> *My sister is a working mom of a couple of children, and yet, she does the cooking, cleaning, managing of the household, transporting kids to places, sewing costumes for dancing, emptying the trash, loading the dishwasher, and even moving the lawns!*
>
> *I still can't work out if she is a control freak or made herself a happy slave!*

Of all the modern studies undertaken regarding the division of chores at home, one point is still crystal clear. Men tend to work longer hours in the workplace, and women tend to do as much as twice the amount of housework and general chores than their partners. What all our clever research also tells us, is that for a lot of couples, this was never *actually* negotiated and *just* happened. You can see the issue looming after a few years of this, can't you?

Consider the following table. What comes to mind when you think of your role? What about your partner? Who are you more like? Cinderella or Sid the Sloth?

Household duties	Other Chores
✔ Grocery shopping and unpacking	✔ Car maintenance
✔ Cooking	✔ Car purchasing
✔ Laundry	✔ Gardening and lawns
✔ Budgeting	✔ Fixing of appliances
✔ Interior decoration	✔ House maintenance
✔ Garbage emptying	✔ Organizing appointments
✔ General cleaning	✔ Taxes and other mandatory duties
✔ Clothes purchasing and repairing	✔ Paying bills
Family Duties	**Social Responsibilities**
✔ Stay-at-home parenting	✔ Christmas cards
✔ Dropping off and picking up children	✔ Keeping in touch with friends/family
✔ Organizing health and other needs	✔ Providing support to others
✔ Homework of children	✔ Organizing
✔ School-related meetings attendance	✔ Making appointments
✔ Babysitting organization	✔ Sending reminders about various things
✔ Purchasing presents/ Organizing parties	
✔ Ensuring toothbrushing/ baths, etc.	
✔ Taking children to dentist/doctor	
✔ Taking days off when children are sick	

So, now that you had a look, what comes to mind? Are you or your partner doing more than you thought? Do you feel that you or your partner are doing less than initially thought? Are you happy with the way these chores are split in your relationship?

What is Fair?

What a great question. What is indeed fair in relationships? I think the first thing to consider is how much work there is in your family unit in the first place. If it is you and your partner, things might not be too difficult. However, if it is you, your partner, three dogs, two cats, and your in-laws, things may be different. If you and your partner have children, the odds are that there will be lots of responsibilities in your relationship that will be constant. Yes, the never ending chores of morning, noon, and night. So how do we divide them?

1. Skills, Talent, and Preferences

There are things that we like doing, things we do not mind doing, and things we despise doing. If you are lucky, the things you hate doing, your partner does not mind, and vice versa. I think it is a fair and an easy solution if both you and your partner recognize chores that you can take on, and are happy to manage them under your "Mr. Muscles" portfolio. However, if this is not the case, it is helpful to write down a list of chores and responsibilities for your relationship and rate them on a scale from 1 to 3.

1 (Yeah, pick me!) 2 (I'm cool) 3 (I wanna throw up)

Remember what we learned in chapter three about negotiations? This will be important here. The idea is that you would both sit down and *negotiate* to the middle, taking a relatively equal number of tasks you love vs. some you hate. I hope that in the end, you would be able to agree on what is fair and reasonable.

> *My boyfriend and I have been in a relationship for six months, and both being guys, we sort of fought over avoiding the same stuff. In the end, we wrote a list of the things we both hated and both loved to do, and randomly picked. We change every month and so far, it's working out! Though I reckon my dinners are much better than his! He cannot deny my Italian God heritage!*

2. Amount of Existing Work

In today's modern world, partners are generally both involved with other activities. Most partners are working these days, though this may not be the case in all relationships. Things to consider are whether a partner is working, whether a person is committed to other responsibilities, how many people are included in this family, etc. For example, if a partner has a full-time job, and the other partner stays at home, there may be an expectation that cleaning the house and doing house chores is the non-employed person's duty. I think this is common and respectable. Both partners are contributing and helping their family remain balanced. It still is important to be respectful and understanding. For example, if your partner is a stay-at-home parent and has nursed a crying baby all day, it would be cruel and unrealistic to expect the house to be spotless when you get home (and if you thought it should, I suggest you read Chapter 8 again on the realities of parenting).

The reverse also applies. If your partner works 50 hours a week while you work ten, but you wait for him/her to get home to discuss who will empty the dishwasher, you need to reconsider what "fair" means. Finally, there is another common scenario, and that is when both partners work an equal amount of time at their respective jobs, but one partner is the designated cleaner, cook, or laundry slave. Irrespective of genders, age, or status, when both partners work as much as each other, the chores and responsibilities should be split equally. Full stop.

3. Special Considerations

Despite the need to share the household chores equally, it is important to be aware of special considerations. For example, in my family, I rarely cook dinner. My husband gets home at least three to four hours before me, and therefore, it makes sense that he would start dinner to avoid everyone starving late at night. On the other hand, he starts work much earlier than me, and so I would never ask him to get the kids ready before school. That has become my job.

Aside from considerations of timing, there are other factors to keep in mind. Sometimes, there are clear financial differences in the income of partners. Couples may make an arrangement that is based on this clear distinction; it would not be viable for one partner to work less. Couples may decide that with the extra income earned from one partner working overtime, they may be able to afford a cleaner on a regular basis, etc. Finally, there may be physical or mental health issues impacting you or your partner's ability to undertake chores. If your partner recently had surgery, just lost their mother, or is sick, you would not expect them to be as helpful around the house. It is important to remember that you love your partner, even when your house is trashed, and the trashcan is overflowing. It's all in the context (and negotiations).

4. To Nag or to Avoid?

In my experience working with couples in therapy, a lot of partners who do not share household chores well, become resentful and angry towards each other. After a time, we can observe some very clear and common behaviors. It moves between one nagging partner to an avoidant one, repeating the same argument over again. It often sounds like something like this.

"You bloody left the dishes in the sink last night!"

[No response]

"You don't think I am going to be your slave forever?"

[Glances up, then ignores again]

"I better not see dishes when I get up tomorrow" [walks off angry].

The odds are that that person will probably see dishes in the sink tomorrow again. Surprise, surprise. Humans do not respond well when feeling threatened, pressured, or simply annoyed. They respond to the sharing of one's thoughts, empathy, rationale, and manners by... well, let me think about this for a minute. Would this sound like an *I message*, clear facts, a reason, and feedback? Yes, it would. Hopefully, this takes you back to Chapter 2, where we discuss communication skills and the PCiR model. Even when discussing chores, basic communications skills are a must. Imagine the same scenario using the PCiR model;

"I noticed that the dishes had been in the sink all night. I was wondering if we were still able to stick to our chore schedule? It does make a huge difference. Would this be okay with you?"

[looks up and hesitates]

"Thank you, honey, and I swear I won't forget to cook us a super yummy dinner tonight."

[Smirks and gets up to the dishes]

[Partner makes physical contact with lover in an unspoken thank you]

This is all hypothetical, and sometimes it will not work. We will talk more about when things go wrong in Chapter 12. But in the meantime, I challenge you to be aware of nagging and avoidant behaviors. If this is where you are headed, remind yourself of Chapter 2 on communication and start practicing. In the meantime, right now is about negotiating. We have established that household chores and other responsibilities are not the problem of only one partner. These need to be split fairly. How that looks in your relationship is up to you, as long as both partners are happy and comfortable with it. If you need to, go back to Chapter 3 on meeting in the middle, and practice the exercises until you come up with a compromise for the tasks discussed in this chapter.

→ Chapter 9 Tips ←

Decide on What is Important. Not all couples have the same priorities. For examples, in my family, we rarely iron and when we do, it's probably to go to a wedding or a funeral. However, I am well aware that in other relationships, ironing is a huge priority, and therefore, it is about being aware of these needs. Sometimes, a priority will be different for one partner and the other. It is unrealistic to expect your partner to take the lead over a task they do not value, as long as it is not a vital chore. If they do not value basic hygiene, then forget this last sentence. Couples should discuss the important tasks and responsibilities, and look at how the rest can be left out or delegated.

> *When our first child was born, we both decided that that kid needed everything organic and homemade. It lasted nine months before we were yelling every weekend as we were fighting over our budget (do you realize how much organic vegetables actually cost?), who was going to peel, cook, and blend the purees, and then pack and freeze them for another week. Then one day, our pediatrician told us that there was no evidence that kids who ate organic were healthier! So, we stopped. And swapped 6 hours of puree making with 6 hours of family time every weekend. Brilliant!*

Do Not Start Bad Habits. It is extremely hard to stop bad routines once they have commenced. If you have been the family slave for 12 months, and suddenly no longer want to be Cinderella, your partner may not be happy to come to the party initially. No one can take on all the chores and responsibility forever, or at least not without growing resentful or burned out. Start with good habits. Discuss roles and responsibilities from the beginning and negotiate tasks well so that both of you are happy and able to sustain them over time. If you have started bad habits, stop now and talk to your partner about how you are feeling. If you are the partner of someone who has taken on too much, it is in your best interest to take on a fairer amount, if you want your relationship to be happy, healthy, and survive long term.

Contract Out. My husband and I contracted out our cleaning in the last three years. While it is a financial commitment, it is worth every penny. Delegating chores can give you time and energy for other important things, such as family time, bonding experiences, work, rest, and other commitments. Simply put, there are only 24 hours in a day, and most times, we cannot fit it all in the one timeframe. If you are in a position where chores and responsibilities are taking a toll on your relationship, and you can afford it, consider paying someone to help out.

It's Not Always Your Way. Multiple therapy clients who have come to me were upset that they were holding too many responsibilities in their relationship, yet could not allow their partner to do any chores their way. Comments like "he doesn't do it properly," "I need to be able to make sure it is done on time," or "it's just easier if I do it" are extremely common in my experience. However, this usually reflects an element of control and power, which only makes both partners unhappy. If your partner does things differently, then accept his or her approach. If your lover genuinely does not do a good job, do not do it again after them. This is Behavior Modification 101. If you take over for your partner every time they do not meet your standards, then you will, indeed, be doing everything on your own forever. Instead, politely reflect on the objectivity of your concerns, and then show your partner what worries you. For example, you may show

how they could do it differently, but in the end, they should be the ones "fixing" the chore.

Be Flexible. Imagine that you have agreed that this month, you will be doing the floors while your partner will be doing the dishes. No cleaning bible dictates when and how housework should be done. For example, some people may be early risers and believe that cleaning should be done in the morning. Others are night owls and may choose to clean before bed. These are preferences that are neither right or wrong. In the same way, your partner may have a breakfast meeting and decided that the dishes would be done after work. While it may annoy you, be flexible. If the dishes are getting done today, I am sure you can survive a few hours.

Consequences. One of the most frequent questions I get during couple therapy is, indeed, about what should happen if an agreed rule is not followed. Every case is different, but I would like to invite you to reread the exercise on boundaries from Chapter 5. Without a natural consequence, there are no boundaries. However, setting consequences between equal adults can be tricky. The first step might be to agree amongst yourself on consequences. What should happen in one partner does not do their chores? Should the other partner get $50? Should the partner leave the chore undone until it gets done? I do not know, but it is important that consequences are realistic, able to be followed through, and suit your relationship. What might be a consequence for me, may not be realistic for you, and vice versa. However, it is important to discuss issues when they occur as opposed to taking over your partner's responsibilities or nagging him or her without substance and results.

In Summary

This chapter touched on the very real issue of chores and responsibilities in relationships. What I have noted in both my personal and professional experiences, is that duties and obligations change across the lifespan. The way relationships work together also develops over time. What may seem a huge topic of discussion and commitment in the first year of your relationship will not be so after 20 years. So don't let the day-to-day toil impact on the quality of your partnership. The same applies if you have children. The work associated with families is incredible but does not last forever. Therefore I invite you to look beyond the hard work and focus on the rewards. Good communication and negotiations make good and healthy relationships. Be fair and be helpful, and I guarantee you more drive for all the rest.

CHAPTER 9: TRUTH OR DARE

✔ Write down a list of all the chores and responsibilities that are relevant to your relationship. Then score them from 1 to 3 (look up the exercise in this chapter) and classify them in the 1, 2, and 3 columns. Look at which chores are easy for you versus difficult for your partner, and start filtering the easy ones to negotiate.

✔ Discuss the chores that neither of you wants to take on. Write down three options to push the negotiations forward. Some suggestions may include what you would be prepared to do to avoid one chore, how often would you like to swap it, how you would like to do it, or whether you would rather hire someone to get rid of that chore altogether.

✔ If your partner is sick, unwell, or going through something difficult, consider being kind, flexible, and helpful. What would that look like in practice?

✔ Together with your partner, sit down and discuss reasonable consequence for either of you if chores do not get done. These cannot be violent or illegal.

✔ Imagine that your partner did not do their allocated chore for a week. How would you practice the boundaries exercise? What kind of positive natural consequence can you think of?

✔ Gift your partner with a cleaning voucher or a home coupon (or similar) to be used for a chore of his or her choice for their birthday, anniversary, or another occasion.

✔ When things appear difficult (if you are at a stage of life where there are lots of chores and responsibilities), draw how wonderful your life will be in ten years' time, as your chores decrease. Draw strength and patience from friends and family who have gone through it.

PART FOUR

Alone
at Last!

DATING AND KEEPING THINGS ALIVE

Good relationships are amazing. If you are as lucky as me, your relationship with your soulmate is supportive, dedicated, fun, sexy, and evolving. However, when I say evolving, I'm being a little cheeky. I am thinking of the best behaviors both my husband and I would be on, when we first met, and how it gradually changed over the last couple of decades. Things like the clothes we wore (Heaven forbid not wearing matching colors), our grooming and appearances (I swear, my husband carried his secret commercial-size perfume tank), the food we ordered (if it didn't fit into a lady-like spoon size, I did not have it), and our approach to issues, chores, and complaints sure have *evolved* in that time, from the timid "would you mind" to the dragon tone of "do it or else." I suspect that many of you will recognize the subtle changes your relationship has undertaken since you became a couple. In short, how it may now be easier to forget the matching socks, the morning breath, and how swallowing a giant burger in less than a minute can create an explosion of sauce all over your face.

In all seriousness, this chapter is about finding a healthy balance between being the fake-perfect-self that we seem to be in the early stages of dating, to keeping things alive through your relationship over time. Early relationships come with adrenaline, excitement, and passion while long-term ones bring a depth of commitment, genuine trust, and security. As couples become more familiar, they no longer need to look their best or prove their worth. Simply put, it's in the bag, and so we slowly get swallowed by the mundane and day-to-day relationship, and family dynamics.

Consider your relationship. How many efforts go into your appearance and grooming (and I am not talking about the way you dress to go to a work meeting)? What kind of conversations are you having, outside of chores, bills, and children? How would you describe your relationship? Is it more dull and boring, or fun and exciting? Is it an extension of what it used to be or has it completely died down to leave you both feeling disconnected romantically?

I believe that relationships do, and should, change over time. I genuinely think that couples who have been together for 30+ years have stopped having sex on the kitchen counter and most likely no longer cut their toenails behind closed doors. That is what happens when we are comfortable with someone. We start feeling okay as we are, and develop new ways of showing affection. The issue arises when that line is pushed too far and too early. The truth is, as more and more time goes on, the more likely you are to appear a bit looser with some aspect of your relationship. Clothing choices, habits of all kinds, food options, language used, bathroom visits, and bodily function issues will push the boundaries of your romance bible.

> *I remember our first date. My boyfriend had taken me to a burger bar, with little notice. I had no idea about the social norms around that. Clearly stuffing my face with chips and a burger did not match my pretty little outfit. What about paying for the bill? I wished dating came with a guide book before I went out!*

It would be difficult to talk about dating and keeping the relationship alive without mentioning the very famous Gary Chapman's love languages. What we learned from his research is that people communicate in different *love languages*. For example, your partner might love purchasing gifts for you as his or her way to show affection, but may not particularly like receiving them. For him or her, it might be more meaningful to have you spend some quality time with them. You'll find that you will have a couple of ways to show your love, and a couple of different languages to feel loved. According to Chapman, there are five love languages. These are:

1. **Words of affirmation (things like compliments, kind words, little hidden notes in your lunchbox, or a Valentine's Day card).** If words of affirmation are your thing, you would possibly feel very hurt against harsh words and criticism.

2. **Quality time (this would include one-on-one quality time, your partner's undivided attention, common activities, and opportunities to travel together, etc.).** Long periods of silence, and the feeling that your partner values others more, would be hurtful to you if quality time was your love language.

3. **Acts of service** Actions to be helpful, such as emptying the trash, picking up dry cleaning, or giving your partner a foot massage would be meaningful to someone who valued acts of service as a love language. Your partner not helping you at all would be a major turn-off in your relationship.

4. **Physical touch.** Surely this one is self-explanatory. Partners who need physical touch would feel ignored or neglected physically by their lover or would possibly be very touchy-feely towards others.

5. **Receiving gifts.** For those people, receiving presents is a way of feeling appreciated. This may include special occasions or no occasion, but gifts nonetheless. For these partners, the lack of material evidence would be difficult and make them feel undervalued.

> ❝ I can honestly say that prior to that session, I had never heard of the love languages. However, the second I did, it made sense! Suddenly, my love letter thrown sadly on my partner's desk made a lot of sense. I'm glad to say that the chocolate cake I made him the next time was much more appreciated! He still raves on about it!

You may recognize some of the love languages above. You may also note that you or your partner's giving and receiving language may be different. For instance, I might find that gift giving is my way of showing love to those around me, but I *hate* receiving presents. No joke. However, words of affirmation and quality time are the way of making ME feel like a million dollars.

To learn more about the love languages and how to apply them to your relationship, I would encourage you to get a hold of *The Love Languages* by Gary Chapman and indulge in his quiz. In the mean-time, and for this chapter, I would like you to consider the way you receive and reciprocate love. How could you use these strategies while on dates (and through other moments) to make your partner feel special? Create sentimental habits; write your partner love notes and place them in their lunch boxes, dashboards, or bags. You may also want to send them nice texts affirming their strengths for no other purpose than to express your love or include meaningful touches, such as a little treat from the grocery shop as a surprise. It may be a couple of fresh dates, a lollipop, or simply their favorite yogurt. Beware though; being kind just before asking your partner to vacuum the floors will have somewhat less of an impact.

Why Dating?

Many couples think that dating only occurs in new relationships and it should die off once the relationship is official. Not true! In fact, research into couples therapy has shown us that dating in marriage (or de facto relationships) is what keeps the spark alive. The benefits are huge. According to multiple research projects in 2017, couples who continue to date across time feel happier, remain together longer, communicate better, parent more consistently, and have better sex. In my experience as a couples therapist, couples who get stuck focusing on their children, bills, work commitment, and other day-to-day chores, do forget what their relationship is about.

One of my favorite exercises in therapy is to ask partners to engage in a conversation (chosen randomly) for five minutes. It forces partners to practice talking together about a personal topic that is not parenting-work-responsibility related, and while it may sound simple, it is quite difficult when a couple has stopped dating romantically. Consider the following date questions:

- ✔ What is your best memory as a child?
- ✔ Describe your first meeting.
- ✔ Guess each other's favorite meals.
- ✔ Discuss your thoughts about a particular book or movie.
- ✔ Take turns at saying jokes.
- ✔ Share a secret (obviously not a sad secret or the date will be over soon).
- ✔ Describe how you would like to see your lives in ten years.
- ✔ Impersonate a famous person.

- ✔ Recall a dream you had and share it with your partner.

- ✔ Imagine you won 1 million dollars. How would you spend it?

- ✔ Describe a romantic moment between the two of you that turns you on.

These are only samples, and I encourage you to make up your own. The sky is the limit when it comes to conversation starters. The key is in making the topic fun, interesting, and an opportunity to get closer to each other. If you have not practiced this for a while, you may find this extremely difficult. This is normal, but you should make a point of practicing. Dating, connecting, and growing in the same direction together with your partner is what will keep you on a strong relationship path. To assist with successful dating in relationships, here are some of the key ingredients to make it work.

> *Our relationship moved up and down over the seven years we have been together. But if there's one thing that never changed, it is our monthly date. It doesn't matter what it is, if no one's dying, we don't want to hear it. That night is for us and for us only. And it's kept us sane many times!*

First of All, Have Fun

Dating is more than just ticking off a list of "should." Yes, it does make relationships stronger, but not if the dates are boring and filled with arguments. Have fun when planning your outings. Ensure that you alternate between activities that you like with activities that your partner likes. If there are common hobbies you both enjoy, why not make it a regular thing? For example, weekly bowling, monthly camping, Friday movies, or Sunday restaurant outings. There are times where couples do not have the resources to go on regular dates. I remember the times when our children were young, when finding a babysitter was difficult, and when the funds to spend on our date would have taken a chunk out of our grocery allowance. During those times, going *out* at all was not happening. However, what was workable was to rent a movie, maybe even get a special treat (chocolate, popcorn, ice cream, etc.), and to lock the door until the next day. Our dates, and the dates of many young couples I have worked with, may not have been fancy, but they achieved their purpose: connection, peace, time away from the routine, and maybe even some romantic time thrown in there. Remember that it is not what you do, but the opportunity to break the routine and to spend quality time together that counts.

Find new things to try and keep the novelties happening.

Mystery, Attraction, and Sex Appeal

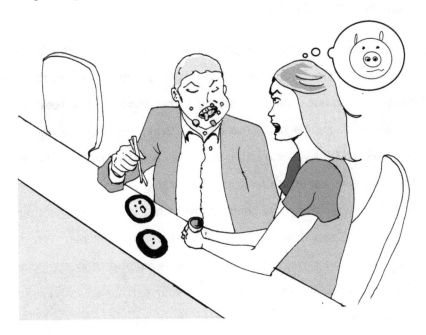

As we discussed earlier, relationships change over time. If you have been with your partner for a while, you may stop looking at him or her the way you did in the first year. While this is normal, I think that part of a good and positive relationship is to keep up the spark. How can you remain attractive to your partner over time, when you live and breathe together a good part of the day? Some may disagree, but I would advise to keep up simple polite manners. For example, I recall a couple I once knew who had been together for 20 years. One of the partners would fart at the table every day, to the great laughter of his children. Now, I never found out whether this impacted on his lover and the way people living with him saw him, but I would guess it would be tricky to visualize warm and passionate embraces with someone who regularly shares pretty graphic bodily functions.

Now, do not get me wrong. In no way am I implying that long-term couples would be able to hide basic human behaviors from their partner, but what I am saying is that there is a line between regular habits and purposely oversharing them with someone who is supposed to find you attractive until the day you die. In addition to this, make a point to look nice for your partner on your dates. Not only does this help to romance over time, but it's also sending a message to your lover, "yes, I still want you to want me." When they dress up for you, give them compliments and show appreciation. Sex appeal is as much about how your partner sees you, as it is about the way you feel about yourself.

> *I dated this girl once, when I was 20. Holy cow, she was something. And by no means am I sexist in any way, but there are definitely things that will turn off any guy. We went out for dinner and had a great time. We went back to her house, and at some point, she called me into her bathroom. Here she was on the toilet, clearly taking a dump with all the associated smells and noises, asking me for company because she was bored. The second she started wiping, I was out of there and never turned back. I heard she's still single!*

The Most Important Things: Respect, Commitment, and Friendship

In my therapeutic work, I have come across couples who went out religiously on weekly dates every Friday night, because someone told them to, and yet could not stand the sight of each other. They would order movie tickets routinely, not speak during the car trip, watch the movie, and make their best effort to appear like a great couple if they ran into acquaintances. This is a complete waste of time and money. Dating is meant to be an opportunity to give you and your partner the chance to break away from the regular stresses of day-to-day life, and to give you both the chance to reconnect. However, it is hard to reconnect with someone with whom you have spent the last five days visualizing under a bus.

Relationship quality is not just about the weekly date you might implement. It's about the depth of your connection, and the amount of respect and trust you have for each other. It's also about friendship and the fun, dreams, and goals you might share. If you lack in these, make a point of working on them first. Getting along and nurturing a friendship is the first step to being long-term lovers.

Be selfish; prioritize your "us" time. Invent dates that suit the budget and schedule, and ensure that you show kindness and gratefulness in-between moments. Your relationship is worth investing in.

→ Chapter 10 Tips ←

Take the Initiative. Dating is important and awesome. It provides couples with something to look forward to and a platform to rekindle their passion on a regular basis. However, at different stages of life, one or the other partner may be busier or more preoccupied than the other. Things like health, parenting, finances, work issues, and other personal matters may mean that at some point, one partner is in a better position to organize and implement your dates. Do not get stuck on the notion that is it one partner's role to facilitate them all the time. Take the initiative. Be creative. Focus on the fun part, rather than the process. If after ten years you find that either you or your partner have never organized or valued your date, then maybe it might be worthwhile exploring. In the meantime, enjoy the moment and the opportunity to take turns at surprising each other.

Show Appreciation. Say thank you for both the big and little things. At times, certainly in long-term relationships, it is easy to forget what our partners may do for us, and appear almost ungrateful. It is important to show how grateful you are, as it not only is kind and contributes to a healthier relationship, but it also is basic positive reinforcement. If you want your partner to continue being kind, attentive, helpful, etc., you will need to make it worthwhile and let them know how awesome they are. Couples who feel appreciation towards each other feel more content and have better marital satisfaction, so more reasons to be thankful.

Be Holistic. Consider your partnership over multiple aspects. You may be intellectually stimulated by your partner, but find that you are completely disconnected physically. The opposite may apply; you may find that you are having great sex, but are not able to communicate on any level. Relationships are about lots of things, and we should be working on all facets to be as complete as we can. What areas of your relationship are you pleased with? Are there any areas you would like to work on? What are these? You may want to include these areas in your dating as to improve those areas and to feel connected on lots of levels with your partner. Areas may include physical, spiritual, intellectual, sexual, emotional, and practical. I have yet to meet the perfect couple, and it is unlikely that couples could feel fulfilled in *all* areas of life. However, being aware of these strengths and weaknesses in your relationship may give you some ideas for relationship building.

In Summary

You may associated dating with what you do at the beginning of a relationship. What we have established, though, is that dating is the best part of any relationship, forever. Being connected to your partner, particularly if you have heavy work or parenting commitments, is the only way to remain on the same wavelength over the years as life takes a toll on your body and mind. When I talk about dating, what I am talking about is our ability to show kindness, interest, and attention in both body and mind to our partner. Make the time to look your best for him or her (of course, this is subjective. I am not asking you to wear leather pants and carry a whip), treat him or her better than you would treat strangers, and consider your journey as a couple. The closer you are growing up together, the better your relationship will be when you find yourself finally alone and in peace on your porch as you approach your well-deserved retirement.

CHAPTER 10: TRUTH OR DARE

✔ Print the conversation starters from this chapter (as well as any others) and cut them individually. Randomly pick one, with your partner, and practice holding a conversation on that topic for a set amount of time.

✔ Write your partner a thank-you note for something they did. Write it from your heart and give it to them.

✔ Search for Gary Chapman's love language quiz and do the test. Discover your different love languages and discuss with your partner. Are you surprised? How will you use this knowledge now?

✔ Take turns at organizing a date with your partner. Make sure it is something new and fun. It does not have to be expensive, but it needs to be thought through.

✔ Ask your partner what makes them feel connected to you. This should include multiple areas, such as physical, emotional, sexual, and intellectual, etc.

✔ Together, write a list of date ideas. Put them in a jar and pull one out every time you are unsure of what to do/ where to go on your next date.

✔ Consider your outfit/presence for your next date. How could you make yourself look your best for your partner?

✔ Consider any habits you might have, which may be huge turn-offs. For Heaven's sake, get rid of them.

SEX AND INTIMACY

Welcome to a very interesting chapter on how to introduce sex toys, whips, floggers, and kink into your sex life. Just joking! There is absolutely nothing wrong with enjoying sex toys with your partner, of course. The first part of this chapter will be about promoting intimacy—that bond of closeness with your partner that allows you to share thoughts, trust, acceptance, and deep love. The second part will discuss sex across your relationship cycle and provide some tips as to how to keep things alive and exciting over the years.

For many people, intimacy and sex go together. Ideally, this is truly the best combination and something I wish for all of you. Imagine this perfect picture: you and your partner, having amazing sex as often as you want and until your 90s, preceded and followed by feelings of respect, trust, warmth, and love. Yes, and yes again! Unfortunately, as we read throughout this book, there are unavoidable rollercoasters in relationships that may impact on your sex life and intimacy. Pregnancy, parenting, workload, financial stress, arguments with friends or family, as well as communication issues can impact on the quality of your bedroom connection.

Let's start by looking at the distinction between sex and intimacy. Can people be intimate while not sexual, or be sexual without being intimate? The answer is a definite yes.

> *I knew my partner was the one after we had sex for the first time. I'd had sex before with other partners, but never like that. Never in a way that I felt connected to someone else on such a visceral level. I felt completely and emotionally swallowed by my lover. Like I had fully surrendered myself to him in this huge bubble of trust and safety. I still have goosebumps talking about it!*

On the Craft of Authentic Intimacy

Intimacy is about your emotional bond. How close do you feel to your partner? Can you talk about your deep dark secrets? Do you feel like you could trust your partner implicitly and them, you? Are you willing to give yourself fully to your lover and be vulnerable with them? If the answer is yes, you are likely quite intimate with your partner already. In practice, this is shown through gentle approaches and communication, good connections in the way partners understand each other and relate together, and through physical touches, such as strokes of the hand, kisses on the forehead, or warm embraces.

Sex can be very intimate. However, it also can be just that: sex. It is not uncommon for new or short-term partners, who either do not know each other very well or have just met, to have sex in a way that is controlled, emotionless, or free from giving away any personal vulnerabilities. Now, there is no law that says that sex cannot be enjoyable in this way, but we do know that sex and intimacy together make for a hell of a better time, particularly for serious relationships. There are three principles to start developing intimacy with your partner.

1. Appreciate Yourself.

It is hard to be comfortable in bed with your lover if you are completely focused on all the things you hate about yourself. After all, keeping the lights turned off so that your partner won't look at your thighs, your red cheeks, or the way you move during the act is likely to be a buzzkill for both of you. However, liking yourself goes beyond the physical. A healthy outlook on you as a person, and a nice dose of self-esteem, are what will allow you to be vulnerable with someone else. If you have not accepted yourself for who you are, make it a priority.

2. Trust and Affection.

As much as it is hard to be intimate with someone when we feel uncomfortable about ourselves, it is even harder to be intimate with someone we do not trust. Intimacy, like trust, can take time to build. However, if you are in a relationship without trust, willingness to listen, compromise, and genuine affection, things may not be as warm as you'd wish. It is important to work on trust and connection in your relationship so that intimacy builds itself over time naturally.

3. Clear and Honest Communication.

Remember how I said that communication was the most important part in relationships? This applies here also. Clear and honest communication with your lover allows you to know where you stand, predict reactions, and learn more about yourself and your partner. Things like body language and non-verbal cues guide you both in what is working, and not working, in your relationship. That level of understanding, particularly when it is non-threatening and warm, leads to feelings of trust, respect, and therefore, deep intimacy.

> " *I remember having this one-night stand once, and while it wasn't bad, it wasn't great either. All I kept thinking was that his name was Bert, like in Sesame Street. I spent the whole night visualizing his stripy jacket and how I was sleeping with a puppet. The next morning, his mother walks in and called him "Mike." His name wasn't even really Bert!*

The way I look at it, intimacy in a relationship is two people sitting on a porch in silence, feeling completely comfortable with it and each other. It's two people lying in bed, murmuring, "I love you" after they've made love, and as they're falling asleep in each other's arms, feeling safe. It's a lover walking past his or her partner, slowly brushing their hand against theirs as they walk past. Intimacy is the secret ingredient to make your couple and your sex life as good as it can be. However, even with intimacy, sometimes sex can take a back seat, particularly when there are competing priorities.

Sex across the Seasons

All of us reading this book will be at different stages of our relationship. Some of us will have been together for decades while others will only have been together for months. Some will have children, while others won't, and some will be in crisis while others will be enjoying blessed days on paradisiac islands. It is easy to see how stages in our relationship will influence how we enjoy sexual intimacy. For example, the young couple who has been together for a year will likely have more time and energy for sex compared to another young couple with two children and who are stressed out of their minds about their unpaid mortgage. Age, health, stress, time, and relationship issues can impact on sexy times. Let's take a quick look at those.

- ✔ **Mental Health.** A person in four will suffer from mental health ups and downs. Consequently, the odds are that one of you will develop mental health issues during your life. Before you all start saying "hell no," let me reassure that it is a definite "hell yes." Consider mental health on a continuum, as you would physical health. There are good days, and there are bad days, and none of them are life sentences. It's just life. When one of you isn't doing so great mentally, you may not feel like having wild sex (or who knows; you might want it more).

- ✔ **Stress.** We discussed stress, chores, and responsibilities earlier in this book. When lovers are preoccupied with things that are causing them anxiety, stress, or worries, they may not be completely present in body and mind. This can also affect whether sex is on the list of priorities (though, I must add that it has been recommended over the centuries for stress relief). For most people, this generally subsides once the stress improves.

- ✔ **Time Constraints.** You may be physically supercharged for hot sex, but little Jimmy has not shut up for the last four hours, or you only have ten minutes between coming home and leaving again for your next meeting.

Or even better, your mother-in-law just turned up, as she does every Sunday, guided by her anti-sex radar, and there goes another week. Alright, this may be a little far-fetched, but you get the idea.

> *It took me a while to put two and two together, but it turned out that the best sex we ever had was on Friday nights, after my wife came home from work to a very clean house. It started out by me just being proactive, but ended with me cleaning in view of the predicted reward!*

✓ **Age.** There are known biological changes with aging. However, being older does not mean you are dead. Many older couples continue to enjoy a sex life into their retirement, and while it might be slower and possibly less active, they often described it as satisfying nonetheless. The two main concerns described by older partners are erectile dysfunction and menopausal dry spells. However, there are likely other health issues that may piggyback onto these. With age comes illnesses, such as diabetes, heart disease, arthritis, and even cancers that may impact on lovers' physical ability to perform and their libido. Understanding how you can accommodate these may be the first thing to consider.

Debunking the Myths

In my experience as a couples therapist, and as someone often engaged in sex therapy with clients, there are common myths that creep up in people's minds when it comes to intimate relations. For example, if you think of sex, what are some of the stereotypical comments that come to mind? Are those evidence-based or are they simply ridiculous? What happens though, when couples believe them? How does their sex life change based on perceptions originating from Grandma's tales? What I have learned over the years in therapy, is that both men and women can be influenced by these thoughts, and being able to challenge them is a good way to debunk them. Let's have a look at some of the common ones:

- ✔ **Men want sex all the time.** Here is where I watch you yell "bloody oath they do," but hear me out. See, while it might be true that some men may be sexually driven, particularly between 15 and 25, you can imagine how the partner of a male, whose lover does not need daily sex, may feel. I have worked with countless men and women, all partners of males, who felt devalued, rejected, misunderstood, and unloved, because their partner did not need sex as much as they thought he *should*. After all, men want sex all the time. This myth completely rejects the notion that men are human, and equally impacted by health, stress, and time constraints. If your husband or boyfriend does not jump on you every five seconds, it does not mean that you are unwanted. It simply means your lover is a human and not a machine.

- ✔ **Good girls don't ask for sex.** This is another interesting concept that impacts on relationships. Imagine that you were raised religious, conservative, or simply surrounded by clear messages that women asking for sex was either slutty or desperate. How would you feel about taking the first step in the bedroom, or having a female partner who is forthcoming with what she likes? It would not be unusual in these circumstances for a partner to either feel that they should contain their sexual needs or for a lover sharing these mythical thoughts to be uncomfortable in the relationship. Let me be clear right now; this is where intimacy is incredible. With a partner that you trust, love, and can be yourself with, you should be able to ask anything and feel completely okay with it (clearly, as long as it's within the realm of two consenting adults).

✔ **A low sex drive means there is a problem.** Another common one. Having a low sex drive as a couple isn't good or bad. It clearly does not define your relationship, but may highlight anything from stress and preoccupations to health and hormonal issues. At times, relationship difficulties impact on a couple's sex drive. It is understandable that if lovers are on a warpath, they may not be interested in connecting sexually. However, for other couples, they may be happy having very fulfilling sex once a month. It's all in the context.

✔ **Spontaneous sex equals the best sex.** This one is a common one in couples under 45. There is this fantasy that sex should be spontaneous, passionate, and completely off the chart every time. Come on, people, consider the excitement of knowing that this afternoon, you will engage in a sensual session, filled with intimacy, discovery, and tantric touches (we will discuss sensual mindfulness later in this chapter) that will be all about taking your time and enjoying your lover. How can you tell me that anticipating all of this would *kill* the romance? Absolutely not! The best sex is the one where you are connected to your partner in mind and spirit, regardless of whether it is spontaneous or anticipated.

> *I just couldn't get past the fact that it wasn't about me. When all my friends whined that their partners wanted it all the time, I was faced with a man that was content with a once-a-fortnight regime. Once I accepted that it had nothing to do with me, and everything to do with stereotypes, we were both fine!*

On the Road to a Satisfying Sex Life

Imagine that sex is a journey. While it ends with orgasmic bliss, it is filled with sexual tension, teasing, foreplay, respect, trust, and affection along the path. In some ways, the way to forge good sexual chemistry starts much earlier than in the bedroom (or in the kitchen, car, or bathroom). Being connected with someone sexually requires you to be connected emotionally, spiritually, and physically. So how do we make this happen?

Flirt. Despite what the movies may try to tell us, flirting is not reserved for teenagers or single girls looking for a free milkshake. Flirting implies an element of playfulness, even between partners. What that looks like in your relationship is up to you, but why not throw in there some batting eyelashes, slow undressing, and sensual tones? On a more serious tone, make flirting a part of your routine with your lover. Attract, entice, and reward each other with a playful and exciting prelude. It will only add to both your excitement and sexual experience.

Spice Things Up. At times, sex with long-term partners can become routine. There are lots of ways to spice things up. This could include anything from different clothing, new haircuts, and a change of scenery, to sexy underwear, sex toys, and even roleplaying. There is no right and wrong in the way we spice things up with our partner, as long as both of you are happy with the ideas (though, clearly if you decide to walk around naked and have sex in your local park, you may quickly encounter a problem).

Communicate. I cannot say this enough. Communication is the key to successful relationships. This also applies to sex. What is it that you enjoy or dislike? Have you let your partner know that when he or she kisses your foot, you want to run away and hide? What about asking them for what feels good, or would be exciting to them? Don't be shy. Apply the communication strategies we discussed in Chapters 2 and 3 and go for it. Talk to each other about your sexual fantasies.

Happy Together. I believe it is hard to have a genuine sexual connection with someone we do not like. If your partner is driving you up the wall, and you have found yourselves on the verge of separation, clearly sex may not be the best experience for either of you. While lots of people have sex without feelings (and that may even be great sex), being happy with someone makes sex much more rewarding. Consider all aspects of your relationship. Are there things you could be working on? If yes, work on them. Even working on chores together can improve your sex life. Try it. I am not lying.

Be Active and Rested. This one sounds a bit silly, but hopefully, you will see my point in just a minute. Imagine that you planned on this great sex adventure, but after five minutes, your heart can't take it, your legs are sore, and you've stopped feeling your arms. There is nothing wrong with taking a break. Being physically active and well-rested will help your endurance, performance, and your ability to enjoy the moment. You do not need to be an athlete to have sex (obviously, or half of us would be asexual). But you do need to have a level of health and fitness. Next time you're avoiding the gym, remember the connection between good sex and fitness.

Make the Time. Sometimes, sex is the last thing on our mind. We may have genuine competing priorities, and sex does not fit into our busy schedule. People have found that making the time is important. It may feel like an inconvenience for the first five seconds, but generally, once couples have engaged in lovemaking, the grocery list and dirty dishes go out the window. So, make the time, even if you have to schedule it in. While it sounds bizarre, the more you prioritize a healthy sex life, the easier it will fall into place on its own.

Mindfulness and Sex. If you Google "tantric sex," "sensate focus exercises," or "mindful sex," you will come across a load of exercises and challenges to make lovemaking an amazing experience. Things like noticing smells, touches, movements, body shapes, and heart rates help us feel much more connected to ourselves, and much more aware of what is happening in the present. In addition to this, I have often taught these exercises in sex therapy with clients, particularly when they have had sexual issues in their relationship. This may include touching your partner for a set time without him or her moving, and while taking in the feelings. The game is to avoid jumping into intercourse, but to face thoughts and emotions through the experience, taking turns at touching, and being touched. It's quite intimate.

> The first time I heard about those sensual exercises, I thought they were either for people with issues or for perverts! Then we were challenged to try, so we did!

OMG. It was amazing. It was also very emotional and so intense. But OMG. OMG. OMG.

⟶ Chapter 11 Tips ⟵

Schedule Sex Dates. As we discussed above, make the time and plan the right setting. If you're going on a date to a fancy restaurant (or your local diner), why not take a stroll down the beach to connect before going home to a kid-free house (hand off the kids to your parents for the night). Plan quality and uninterrupted time to connect with each other.

Relax the Mood. So, your partner has just come home from work and is still looking at his diary to schedule his or her next meeting. Don't rush but take five minutes to set the mood. Invite your partner to sit on the veranda for a while, get them a drink or snack, and maybe have a hot bath together or cuddle on the couch in front of the TV until you're both more inclined for the next step. Timing is everything.

Sexting. Alright, maybe that one was simply to get your attention. But in all seriousness, I invite you to send your partner messages throughout the day, leaving little notes in lunches or cars to let your lover know you are thinking of them. Maybe send cheeky messages during the day about fantasies or sensual connotations. Get each other in the mood through the day for an even better night.

Hugs and Kisses. Physical contact that goes beyond sex is important. Hugs and kisses are a positive way to connect partners. Nothing like hugging in bed, feeling embraced in the arms of your lover, or resting your head on your partner's chest, listening to their heartbeat. Make an effort to give each other hugs and kisses, though I must warn that being cued in your partner's body clock is a smart move. Don't decide to hug them when they are in the middle of something important or needing space from the world.

> *The fun thing about sexting is that I would never do it face-to-face. But behind my little screen, I feel okay being naughty. My partner loves it and it makes a hell of a fun time when we get home. Once I even broke my record and sent a photo! I hope our children never go through our phones! Ha, they think we only had sex to make them!*

In Summary

It is difficult to condense such an important topic in one chapter; however, I hope that this chapter will give you some thoughts regarding sex and relationships. Sex can be amazing as much as it can be a poor distraction for some. Be aware of what your body and mind tell you and communicate with your lover about what works and does not work for you.

Remember to take the pressure out. No sexual relationship is the same. While you may have sex three times a week, others may only have sex once a month. Sex is not about how often you do it or how long you do it for; it's about how well you connect to your lover and how intimate you may feel together.

At times, sex is difficult. It may trigger negative feelings, feel unnatural, or simply may not occur at all. Sexologists and couples' therapists who are interested in sexology are available, and I invite you to seek support if you are not having an amazing sexual relationship with your lover. After all, we all deserve this.

CHAPTER 11: TRUTH OR DARE

✔ Consider the level of intimacy in your relationship. Sit down with your lover and discuss what would improve your level of intimacy. It may be as small as listening to each other's day, increase physical touches, or being comfortable with each other's silences.

✔ Sit down with your partner and choose a personal topic to discuss. Practice authentic listening, caring, and loving-attention giving. Notice how you feel safe and trusting (if you don't, go back to the chapters on communication and dating), and describe these to your special person.

✔ Plan a sex date. Pick a date, a place, and the perfect setting around it. It might end in a hotel or after organizing a babysitter. Even consider your clothes, grooming, and flirting vibes. Make it awesome.

✔ Text your partner some lovely kind words, maybe laced with some sensual tone here and there. Do not be offended if they cannot reply during their meeting. It's about making them feel special. If you're the partner receiving these hot messages, make a point to reply with an invitation for more.

✔ Write a list of sexual fantasies and share them with your partner. Make it light, playful, and non-threatening. Don't take things too seriously if your partner thinks that sex with disco lights is a turn-on. It's about discovering each other and what gets you both to tick.

✔ If you have had a very average sex life so far, do something about it. Practice tantric exercises, make sex a priority, or see a sexologist. Do it. You won't regret it.

✔ Practice mindfulness. Commit to one touching session, focusing on the present, touches, and feelings, without ending in sex. Notice how it feels and listen to your partner's experience as well. Get to know each other's bodies and reactions. Then have mind-blowing sex, of course.

WHEN THINGS GO WRONG

I have worked with couples for a long time now. As I get to know people's stories, I often think of the simple reasons relationships unravel, and I promise you, often these reasons are insignificant until you put 100 of these together. By then, it hurts like a tsunami. It may start with a partner answering their phone a particular way, a lover touching their partner's knees or nose in an annoying manner, or differences of opinion about bills, home décor, or Christmas parties. In fact, I have only facilitated a handful of therapy sessions where partners came to me for a *real* reason (though it happens and often relates to grief, trauma, and specific incidents). Most of the time, couples see me to find a way out of their self-made tsunami of resentment, left festering over a long period.

When I meet new clients for the first time in counseling, I ask the same loaded question at the end of the session; "Do you want to make things work?" Sometimes, I may ask whether the partners love each other, or whether they would like to stay together. No matter how I word it, the key question here is how committed the couple might be in working hard at getting back on the love track.

Some of you may think that it is a very stupid question. In some ways, yes, it is; until couples look at me and tell me that they would rather stick hot needles in their eyes than to picture their retirement with the person sitting next to them. Then, it becomes a valid question. How can anyone or anything make a couple improve their relationship when they do not want this to happen?

However, with willing participants, I believe that relationships can recover from most of the common relationship trials. First of all:

1. **Are both partners safe?** As a social worker by trade, I have witnessed my share of domestic violence and deadly substance use. The first question is whether a person wants to change. Without this, forget it. The second question is whether both partners are safe during this transition. Please, do not ever think that it is okay to be at risk, unsafe, or hurt, for the sake of working on your relationship. Sometimes, we want to change but are not capable without great support. My advice here is to acknowledge both of your safety. If your safety is not guaranteed, then relationship improvement should not be the priority.

2. **Are both partners willing and able to work on their relationship?** As above, there is only so much we can do with one or both partners unwilling to be in a relationship. If you happen to be in a relationship with someone who genuinely wants out, consider focusing your energy on grieving and accepting a civil separation. Bluntly, you cannot force someone to be with you.

3. **Does the couple have, or are willing to accept, support and tools to improve the relationship?** If the answer is yes, woohoo! If no, consider that there are lots of tools, exercises, and advice that professionals can give. Also, it is human nature to behave differently in front of a third party, and so you may find it easier to communicate with a mediator about your relationships difficulties.

> *I remember that first session and the question as to whether we were truly wanting to stay together. I think that having to hear the question and having to answer it, sort of made us realize that we were at a crossroad. When I heard that my partner could not imagine us living separately, my heart melted!*

Other factors influence whether partners survive relationship ordeals. Resources, love, commitment, respect, support, personality and temperament, perception, and resilience are some of those. Everyone faces hardship and trauma through their lives. I have yet to meet a couple who can say that they have not encountered their share of issues (unless they're 20, living rent-free, and have no children, with a maid). Whether it relates to issues about physical or mental health, work or studies, shattered dreams, or simply an unforeseen event, we are bound to be tested over time. The way we face these difficulties is guided by how *resilient* we are. *The Healthy Mindsets for Super Kids* (Jessica Kinglsey Publishers, 2013) is a good program to understand the basis for resilience. While I designed it for children, it explains that resilience allows us to respond to stress positively or negatively. It permits us to bounce back from tribulations in a way that lets us recover from them.

How does one become more resilient? Ideally, resilience is built upon in childhood (get your copy of the *Healthy Mindsets* book). Communication skills, social skills, distress tolerance, positive perceptions of events, and healthy self-esteem are a good start. However, adults can build on their resilience, both as individuals and as couples. Here are some ideas to build your resilience through relationship issues:

- ✔ **Self-Care.** By having a healthy dose of good support, access to "me time," and prioritizing your own needs and goals, you are less likely to feel resentful and upset. Self-care allows us to feel nurtured and revitalized on a regular basis and stops burn-out (yes, you can get burned out, even in relationships). Self-care could be anything from a bubble bath, healthy eating, good sleeping, to treating yourself to a haircut.

- ✔ **Surround Yourself with Support.** Whether from friends, family, or professionals, having support is vital. It allows us to voice thoughts out loud, get objective opinions (hopefully), normalize how we feel about our issues, and vent (who can tell me that venting does not feel good?). Find positive friends and good listeners who can listen and share their positive vibes on the topics.

- ✔ **Perspective, Perspective.** If you follow me on Facebook, you'll know about my weekly positive-psychology challenges. What worked well this week? What are you grateful for? Name three things you are looking forward to this month, or list things you are proud of yourself for. These are all helpful in building a positive outlook on life. For example, if your partner betrayed you when he or she forgot your anniversary, you are likely to be upset, angry, or cold. If you consider that you guys just had a baby or are short in money, or you decide to organize something yourself, you are likely to feel better about it. Having a positive outlook on life and your relationship is going to make it better, I promise you.

✔ **Relax.** When couples go through relationship issues, they are likely to take things personally, overreact, jump to conclusions, respond with anything but an assertive tone, purposely leave out their partner's underwear out of the washing load, and lace their soup with laxatives. Just kidding! That last one is a no-no. However, yes. Partners who are going through difficult times can become unpleasant, and the whole relationship can become a "tit for tat," meaning it becomes about being right, settling scores, and paybacks. And guess what? This does not help relationship building. So, cut it out.

When working on rebuilding strength in your relationship, think of it as giving work colleagues feedbacks on their performance. There's no way you would come out and say, "man, you are crap at your job" (or if you would, hopefully, you are not their manager). In all professionalism, you are more likely to point out how well they cleaned the floors, how bright the windows look, and only then mention that they may need to focus on the cleanliness of the tables. This way, the person would accept their limitation while focusing on their successes too (remember how we talked about self-esteem and hope having an important part to play in healthy relationships?). There is no way that you or your partner would work hard at relationship building if all you heard were critiques, negative comments, and hurtful snide remarks. One strategy is to give at least three-to-five positives to your lover before you share one negative one with them. As you share that negative observation, you should still deliver it in a way that is respectful and loving, particularly if your relationship is in a vulnerable stage of the relationship. Consider the following deliveries:

"As usual, you couldn't help but wash all the whites and colors together. It's just plain lazy if you ask me."

vs.

"Thank you so much for doing the washing today. I appreciate coming home, and it's done for us. The towels smell fresh (insert deep inhaling of the fresh towel). Next time, I wonder if we could separate the whites and the colors to see whether it makes a difference in the way they come out. What do you think?"

Surely, you can see how the second one brings together the various techniques we have discussed in the book gently and lovingly? And before I hear, "but I don't want to speak to my partner lovingly," let me remind you that if you are reading this book and this chapter, it is because you have committed to your relationship and to work hard at it. So yes, you have to speak to each other nicely, even when things are not going the best. (Or pack your bags and call it quits. But do not ever think there is a world where staying with someone while being awful to each other leads to happiness and peace of mind.)

> *We were married for eight years and fought for five of those. One day, we decided that we were sick of fighting and split up. Yeah, it was sad for a little while, but in the end, we are genuinely best friends now. These days, I can even pretend that his cooking is good!*

What are the most common relationship destroyers? At the risk of repeating myself, communication ranks pretty high. As Gottman brilliantly explained, the typical communication dooms include criticism, contempt, defensiveness, and stonewalling. (Gottman is a relationship guru who is worth looking up.) What does this look like in practice?

- ✔ **Criticism.** "You never do anything right," "you always forget my birthday," or "you never help around the house."

- ✔ **Contempt.** "If this is what you look like when trying, I'd hate to see what you look like when not trying" or "oh, thanks, a $2 trashy present. You shouldn't have."

- ✔ **Defensiveness.** "You know I'm busy with work and kids. Why do you always give me a hard time about the house not being clean enough for you? Why can't you help more?"

- ✔ **Stonewalling.** (Picture the sound of silence here). Stonewalling is basically when a partner withdraws from the conversation to avoid the dealing with the stress of the conversation and does not engage.

How can couples address these four heavy communication downfalls in their relationship? Here are Gottman's antidotes (though this may be easier to learn and practice with a therapist).

Addressing criticism includes using "I messages" and speaking in respectful and kind words. Be aware of your tone and body language as well.

CRITICISM

"I MESSAGE"

Contempt will be fixed by genuinely reminding yourself about your partner's strengths and showing gratitude for his or her behaviors.

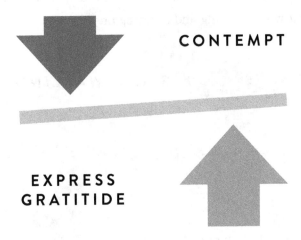

Defensiveness can be lessened by showing accountability in your doings and not jumping to conclusions that your partner is attacking you.

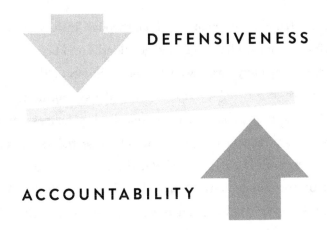

Self-soothing, or finding yourself something calming to do or a positive distraction may help in getting over the habit of stonewalling your partner. It may be helpful to talk to your partner about what upsets you when arguing and agreeing on a break.

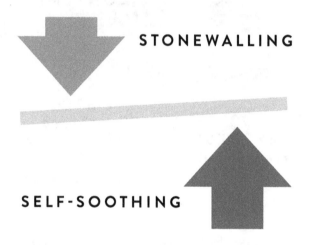

STONEWALLING

SELF-SOOTHING

Quiet Slayers

Most of the tribulations couples will go through include things that are pretty insidious. They come and go silently, and before we know it, we are completely swallowed by them. Some of these include financial stress, bad habits, insecurity, jealousy, taking things for granted, controlling behaviors, negative thinking, laziness, and poor communication. If you recognize any of those habits in yourself, the first step would be to acknowledge these (if you recognize them in your partner, make sure to pass this chapter onto them). Once you identify issues, they are much easier to address. I acknowledge that it is emotional, testing, and draining to work on habits, thoughts, and behaviors that are well-seeded, but it is important if you are serious about improving your relationship. Other times, issues revolve around health, losses, and trauma. These are also important to address at the right time. The following suggestions may help.

- ✔ **Seek Individual Support and Therapy.** You may be well-aware of your own tendency to speak aggressively or to be somewhat selfish (as examples). Seek support if you need to address this. Do not hope that things will change because you wish them to. You need to make the change happen yourself.

- ✔ **Listen to Your Partner.** Men and women process loss and trauma differently. Particularly, health issues may be lived differently for the partner who physically experiences them compared to the partner who is not. It is important to be warm, caring, and to offer a listening ear. Being supportive when things are tough shows that your lover matters. It is easy to be loving and funny when all is going well, but not as deep and rewarding as being kind and compassionate when things are far from well.

- ✔ **Surround Yourself with Positive Vibes.** This includes people, messages, and actions. This will help you share positivity with your partner and focus on uplifting messages, goals, and dreams. Stop seeing your Aunt Betty by herself if all she does is complain about men and makes you see your partner in a dark and gloomy light (or even better, speak to Aunt Betty about focusing on positive conversations from now on).

- ✔ **Be Proactive.** Find solutions to your practical problems. Yes, you have financial stressors, but what about finding ways to increase your income or reduce your costs? What about looking for ways to meet your needs in a way that allows both you and your partner to limit your stress and irritability about the issues. Don't be a victim of life. Be an active participant in its solutions.

> *For us, it was the stress of the kids, work, and the mortgage that slowly drove us apart. There was no big explosion, no major trauma, just slow and progressive hatred of each other. Then we had the car accident and for a minute or two, I thought we would die (we were nowhere near about to die, but I didn't know that, clearly). Our outlook completely changed after that. There was no way we were going to let small, crappy, day-to-day bothers ruin our relationship! Carpe diem!*

Romantic Affairs

Some couples are quite open about involving other people in their relationships, while for others, affairs feel like a complete betrayal. It is important to be clear about what an affair means in your relationship. For many, it is not so much about the act (whatever that act may be), but about the secret behind it. The secrecy and the lies are often more damaging than the kissing, sex, or love exchange with a third party. Here, we are defining an affair as an act that occurs secretly and is hurtful to lovers, as opposed to a lifestyle choice between consenting adults.

Now that the disclaimer is out of the way, let me ask you something. If you considered having an affair, did you discuss it with your partner? If the answer is no, then I assume that it is because, at the back of your mind, you feel it may be wrong. As I said before, I am not saying that open relationships are bad. What I am saying is that both partners have to agree on what this means and entails for their relationship before jumping into a relationship with someone else. If you have considered an affair behind your partner's back, did you hope this would improve your relationship? (Trust me. It is unlikely.) If an affair is your way of forgetting the issues in your current relationship, have you tried to solve your issues more directly? Again, I'm afraid affairs are not the most constructive way of problem-solving disputes with your partner. Things to consider:

✔ **In and Out of Love.** I once heard that relationships were like rollercoasters, with lovers falling in and out of love over and over through their lives together. As we read in this book, there are lots of circumstances in life where partners are stressed, upset, disheartened, and hopeless with each other. Most of the time, the issues are in the circumstances, not with the persons. Give yourself time: time to ride the wave of relationship stress, without trying to run away from it.

✔ **Be Honest with Your Partner.** If things are not going well, let him or her know. Be open to discussing things and resolving them. Consider each other's needs and communicate about your fears, concerns, and wishes, then discuss potential solutions.

✔ **Atone.** If you had an affair, be prepared to accept that your partner will almost always be upset. They may need to ask questions, understand what went *wrong*, and hear you commit to him or her. In short, they may need reassurance that you are, indeed, wanting to work on the relationship rather than believe that you will continue seeking solace in the arms of random strangers.

✔ **Attune.** Once an affair has been disclosed and discussed, there will be work needed in your relationship to rebuild the partnership. If you had the affair, you need to show patience and understanding. Do not rush him or her in "getting over it." If your partner had an affair, be kind to yourself and make sure to work through your thoughts and emotions. It is likely that you may need to speak to an objective third person to help you through it.

✔ **Reattach.** Generally, when a secret affair happens, couples struggle for a while. They may find intimacy and sex difficult, or develop trust issues. It is important to redevelop common goals and dreams again. Learning to recreate intimacy is important, valuable, and an important step for your recovery as a couple. For most people, therapy is very useful.

→ Chapter 12 Tips ←

Whenever my partner annoyed me in the first three years of our relationship, I would fantasize about having a forbidden affair with this hot guy from a TV show. Then one day, my sister reminded me that in real life, even that guy would fart, snore, and probably leave the toilet seat up. I never had any intentions of ever cheating on my man in real life, but after that, even my dreams were PG rated!

Don't Hold a Grudge Forever. No matter what happens in your relationship, do not let resentment eat you up. Like I tell the couples I work with, you either decide to forgive and work hard at it, or you don't. No one can decide that for you, but I guarantee you that staying with a person while swearing that you will never forgive them is a recipe for a very sad life. Either let go of lifelong resentment or let go of your lover. I encourage you to work through your feelings and seek support to be able to do one, or the other.

Treat Your Lover as You Would a Friend. It's a well-known fact that people tend to treat strangers or work colleagues better than family at times. This is because human nature dictates that we keep ourselves on our best behavior until we feel comfortable with the people around us. So, a good rule of thumb for a healthy relationship is to learn to treat your lover better than you would treat your neighbor, for example. Your relationship is important. Nurture it.

Separate the Persons from the Issues. All couples will go through stress, trauma, and issues in their lifetime. This does not mean that either of you are bad people or that your relationship is doomed. Separate the issues from the person. Remember that everyone makes mistakes and whether small errors or bigger life-changing decisions, people have the potential to learn from them. Whether you and your partner learn from them is up to you.

Therapy. Okay, call me biased here, but I am a great believer in therapy and couple counseling. Do not hesitate in seeking support. However, do not feel discouraged if it does not work the first time. Finding a therapist that you gel with is as important as the therapy itself. Not everyone is going to like everyone's style, so find a therapist that you can trust and respect, and go for it. I promise you that couples therapy can make a difference in relationships with big or small issues.

In Summary

As you reflect on your relationship with your lover, you may ponder on great times, and recall some difficult moments. It would be unnatural for a couple not to have experienced trials and challenges. After all, this is what being human means. However, the joys of surviving relationships are being able to recover from the sad parts, while being rewarded with great ones. Resilience, commitment, emotional intelligence, and the access to strategies and techniques like we have discussed in this book will hopefully assist your relationship in riding this crazy rollercoaster.

If you have gone through traumatic events, I am sorry. Please seek support and take care of yourself. If you have not, remember that most separations occur because of day-to-day frustrations. Be aware of the slippery slope of poor communication, loss of respect, and lack of intimacy that slowly creeps up when partners do not pay attention to these gradual changes. Nurturing your relationship with positive and kind words, equal sharing of work and responsibility, and deep intimate connections are the best ways to ensure a fulfilling love journey.

CHAPTER 12: TRUTH OR DARE

✔ Consider your relationship over the last six months. Have things improved, been the same, or declined?

Why do you think this may be the case? Discuss with your partner.

✔ Find three things you could both commit to, to revitalize your relationship. Make the commitment exciting and discuss outcomes in the following month.

✔ List three things that your partner may be doing that annoy you. Put them in perspective. Have these always annoyed you? Or are you focusing on them more?

✔ List three qualities of your partner that you are grateful for. Focus on the positive and remind yourself of these positive aspects of your relationship.

✔ If there are problems in your relationship, start focusing on the issue while removing blame. Together, in a respectful and non-threatening way, work on solving them.

✔ Consider the things you are holding a grudge for. What would need to happen for you to let them go? Is this something that would benefit your couple?

✔ Remember when you met your partner. Write yourself a letter, describing the qualities and events that made you fall in love with him or her. Read it when feeling disheartened.

TOPICS FOR DISCUSSION

Though it may seem old-fashioned, premarital counseling has merit. If you search for "premarital counseling questions," you will stumble on topics that you might find useful to discuss before deciding on the big commitment. Like the chapters in this book, these questions are merely designed to get you thinking about what matters to you, and how you imagine your life to be with your loved one. Having completely different opinions does not mean that you should not be together. It does mean you will need to negotiate things as they arise in front of you. For some, the differences in values, dreams, and opinions will be much too bright, and may lead you to decide that the level of commitment is not right at this time for the two of you. Or who knows? You may find that none of it applies to you and live happily ever after anyway. Either way, I wish you all the best and look forward to hearing about your success stories.

Goals and Dreams

- ✔ What do you hope to achieve in the future?
- ✔ What is important to you?
- ✔ What are your thoughts about religion, values, and traditions?
- ✔ What do you think the purpose of your life is?
- ✔ Where do you see yourself in five or ten years?
- ✔ What kind of work ethic do you follow?

Our Life Together

- ✔ What do you find supportive and helpful in a partner?

- ✔ What are your thoughts about balancing time together and time apart?

- ✔ Where do you want to live? What kind of house, etc.?

- ✔ What are your thoughts about relationships with in-laws?

- ✔ How would you like to celebrate special occasions?

- ✔ How would you share the workload in the household?

- ✔ Who will be responsible for money, budgeting, managing debts, etc.?

- ✔ How do you feel about savings vs. living well?

- ✔ What are your thoughts about alcohol and drugs? When and how often?

- ✔ How do you feel about farting, burping, and various manners?

- ✔ Do you have any health issues (both physical and mental)?

- ✔ Can you think of anything that would be important to share with your partner?

Pregnancy and Parenting

- ✔ When would you like to start a family?

- ✔ How would you manage an unwanted pregnancy?

- ✔ How many children would you like?

- ✔ What kind of discipline do you feel would be appropriate?

- ✔ How do you feel about working parents vs. stay-at-home parents?

- ✔ Who would be responsible for the childcare, taking days off for sick children, etc.?

Conflict Management

- How will you resolve conflict?

- What is your communication style?

- How stressed do you get under pressure?

- What kind of boundaries do you expect when arguing?

- How do you feel about talking to others about relationship issues?

- How would you feel about counseling if you had issues?

Sexy Times

- How often would you like to have sex?

- Are you comfortable talking about intimacy?

- What sexual limits do you foresee (toys, places, particular touches, other people, etc.)?

- How would you talk about sexual needs and differences?

- How important is dating in your relationship?

- What is your love language? What about your partner's? How would you speak each other's language when happy and when stressed?

CHECK-INS

May I invite you to check in on your progress as a couple? Feel free to copy this page and fill it in from time to time. At the time, you may feel it is useless. When you look back, it will bring you lots of surprises as you reflect on the ups and downs in your life as a couple. If not, it can always be an occasion to celebrate your love over time.

Date: _____

Message to myself about this year:

What am I grateful for:

What have I learned this year:

Relationship stressors:

Relationship achievements:

Act of kindness (what will I do to thank my lover for this year's journey):

Goals for next year as a couple:

About the Author

 Dr Stephanie Azri is a Clinical Social Worker with fifteen years of experience in clinical counselling. Her goals are to provide support and services to families experiencing various trials in the form of counselling, advocacy, research, referrals and teaching. Her areas of interests are women's issues as well as intervention in crisis & trauma situations and mental health.

She wrote her first book *High Risk Pregnancy and Foetal diagnosis; Your journey* in 2006 after her third child was diagnosed in utero with Potter's syndrome, a fatal condition. She found that not much was available for families in this situation. Her second book *Healthy Mindset for Super Kids* is a resilience program she also wrote because of her experiences as a mother and after realising the lack of services for children in the community. Her third book *The prenatal bombshell* written with Sherokee Ilse also deals with prenatal issues. She lives in Australia with her husband and their five children.

www.stephanieazri.com

More Books from Praeclarus Press

UNDER ONE SKY
INTIMATE ENCOUNTERS WITH MOMS AND BABIES
BY A BREASTFEEDING CONSULTANT AND NURSE
CHRIS AUER

Under One Sky: Intimate Encounters with Moms and Babies by a Breastfeeding Consultant and Nurse

by Chris Auer

Under One Sky recounts poignant encounters surrounding birth, breastfeeding, and the life circumstances of families from over 77 countries. As a lactation consultant, Chris Auer met with thousands of women as they began their mothering and breastfeeding journey, women from places as diverse as The Congo, Ecuador, Italy, and Nepal, as well as American women from all walks of life. The babies range from healthy, full-term to extremely premature. The mothers range from 12 to 52. Chris Auer has worked passionately to champion mothers on this segment of their life journey. In the retelling of their stories, we see the importance of meeting mothers where they are in the moment, with an accepting, listening presence. *Under One Sky* is beyond a memoir; it's a mosaic of their stories and reveals a poignant picture of our connectedness.

PraeclarusPress.com

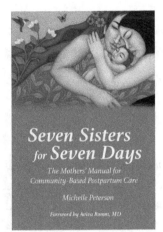

Seven Sisters for Seven Days: The Mothers' Manual for Community Based Postpartum Care

by Michelle Peterson

Many women plan extensively for their birth, and for their baby, but few plan for their self-care in the postpartum period and beyond. *Seven Sisters for Seven Days* is a comprehensive guide book for mothers that illuminates why it is important to receive postpartum care, and how to set yourself up to receive it. This book is an invaluable resource that walks mothers and families through the steps of customizing their postpartum care and teaches them how to call upon a postpartum community care team.

When Postpartum Packs a Punch: Fighting Back and Finding Joy

by Kristina Cowan

When Postpartum Packs a Punch offers solace to mothers who have faced traumatic birth and perinatal mood disorders, as well as a chorus of different voices—parents, experts, and researchers. All are singing the same song: while the U.S. has made strides in caring for new mothers, we still have far to go. Stigma silences women, and blinds those on the sidelines. Stories of others' struggles are an antidote for stigma, because they let mothers know that they're not alone.

Kristina Cowan describes her own experience with traumatic birth and postpartum depression, and weaves it together with stories from other parents. Representing diverse backgrounds and perspectives and underscoring the prevalence of mood disorders after childbirth, these stories serve as a balm. They help heal and stir hope. And they show how an overcoming spirit can fight terrors of the mind—and win.

CPSIA information can be obtained
at www.ICGtesting.com
Printed in the USA
BVHW051200090521
606888BV00018B/1864

9 781946 665195